THE FUGITIVE

LADIN POPOV
with Phil Streeter

ZONDERVAN
PUBLISHING HOUSE OF THE ZONDERVAN CORPORATION
GRAND RAPIDS, MICHIGAN 49506

The Fugitive

Copyright © 1981, Haralan Popov
Box 303, Glendale, CA 91202, U.S.A.

First printing October 1981

Library of Congress Cataloging in Publication Data

Popov, Ladin, 1915-1977
    The fugitive.

    1. Popov, Ladin, 1915-1977.   2. Pentecostals—
Bulgaria—Biography.   3. Clergy—Bulgaria—
Biography.   I. Streeter, Phil.   II. Title.
BX8762.Z8P666   272'.9   [B]   81-16014
ISBN 0-310-44612-0   AACR2

Printed in the United States of America

Contents

Introduction

Within the pages of this book, there nestles the incredible story of a life of suffering and wandering. From childhood to death, Ladin Popov followed the path of problems, pain, and poverty.

From a poor family background, he succeeded in overcoming the dreadful difficulties that plagued the people of his generation.

Ladin was converted on hearing Christ's gospel as spoken by me, his elder brother, Haralan, who at that time was pastor of the Russe Church in Bulgaria.

From that moment on, Ladin's life was shaped in the everlasting things of God. He studied at a Bible College in Danzig and received his ministerial ordination in London. It was here that he fell in love with a girl whom he was never to marry. The suffering of the years threw gigantic canyons of separation between them.

It was as a pastor in Bulgaria that he was arrested, along with fourteen others. By God's power, he remained the only one of that group who refused to yeild to the lies of the Communists.

Through many devious ways they tried to make him admit to espionage, but he resisted— almost to death. The world watched the puppet trial described in this book, and the BBC in England proclaimed him a hero.

Even after his eventual release from prison, life was no easier. Ladin became a fugitive, harassed and chased by the Secret Service for fifteen years until his eventual escape into Scandinavia in 1967.

It was in Sweden that he began a ministry to help those he had left behind. The ministry became known as Evangelism to Communist Lands, a mission that Ladin himself directed, preparing radio broadcasts and tapes, and overseeing the printing of Bibles for free distribution in Communist bloc countries.

Ladin died of a heart attack on June 18, 1977. His life of suffering was obsessed with one purpose—the work of God and the testimony of Jesus Christ. He is now being rewarded by eternal peace and rest in the presence of the Lord. His fugitive days are over.

Haralan Popov
November 1980

Chapter One

"GOOD-BY CITY, GOOD-BY CITY"

I guess it was foolish of me not to have packed my bags and run, but destiny had other things in mind, of which I would never have conceived at the time. Looking back now, I realize that if I had run away, I would have failed miserably in my responsibility to the lonely church at Russe of which I was the pastor. True, I would have escaped the nightmare of communist persecution, but would never have been able to free myself from the haunting of a guilt-riddled conscience. Christ faced death for me—He never ran away. I knew that I had to be prepared to face something similar for Him.

Like a cuckoo laying its rebel egg in another bird's nest, the Communist Red Army, in the winter of 1944, forced its political egg of government on the unsuspecting peoples of Bulgaria. It hatched out, only to be naively tolerated by other political parties even to the extent of forming a coalition government of "friendship"! But baby cuckoos instinctively react to their immediate surroundings by roughly removing all potential hindrances to their total domination of the nest. Unlike cuckoos, however, the communist government was not satisfied merely by having all competitors out of the nest; it adopted the line of total annihilation within the nest itself! And so, with other political parties outlawed and their leaders imprisoned, hostile gaze now turned to the Evangelical Church. I guess we should have ex-

really. People had been flooding into our ...es for many months. There had been con-...ons, mass baptisms, and many miracles—an.. then rumors began! The names of fifteen leaders within the Evangelical Church were systematically smeared with the accusation of spying for Western Imperialist powers. My brother and I were among those fifteen.

It is difficult to exlplain why such governments should become so incensed against the Christian church. Our love for Christ prompted us to help the poor people as well as the rich; we consistently treated all alike; surely communist ideals were similar? After having lived through the inhumane practices of communist ideology I dearly see the reason for the conflict. Many of their leaders were undoubtedly influenced by Satan whose evil strategy is forever opposed to God's love and goodness. It was a case of the wolf putting on sheep's clothing. To begin with, Satan's attacks were ingeniously tempered by the sly cunning of the authorities. Through devious means, rumors were circulated. The faithful members of our churches did not really believe them, but unfortunately few people can consistently remain unaffected by what they hear, even if they are sure it is a lie. Fringe members were quickly taken in and unbelieving members in nearby towns where we witnessed soon became suspicious of our Christian activities.

In 1948 we were warned by the authorities that we must conclude all our correspondence with the West. Presumably they had intercepted our letters; if so, surely they would have perceived that they contained no material suggestive of spying.

Both my brother Haralan and myself had spent one year in Theological College in England, and two similar years at Danzig in Germany (now Poland) as a part of our pastoral training program.

We were not spies; the whole idea was ridiculous. With any communist government, however, falling out with the Party can be disastrous, not only costing people their employment, but sometimes even their lives.

Branded with espionage and our letters banned, the situation became more tense. Many of our friends reluctantly ceased to make contact with us as they gradually became influenced by the lies so cleverly perpetrated by communist authorities.

It was at this time that we heard of several churches where dramatic changes were taking place. Godly men who had served their people for many years were pushed from their position, and others, whom the authorities could easily manipulate, sent to replace them. Inevitably, enthusiasm waned as church activities were curtailed and teaching programs stopped.

It was during this time that my brother Haralan was pastoring one of the largest Evangelical Churches in the Bulgarian capital city of Sofia. On that unforgettable Friday, the 23rd of July, I packed my small suitcase and traveled the one hundred and sixty miles to Sofia, planning to stay with him over the weekend.

Near Sofia were some famous mineral water baths, renowned for their medicinal properties. I decided that I would enjoy their benefits and at the same time try to avoid the crush of the weekend crowds. On Saturday morning I was out of the house just before 4:00 A.M., planning to have my bath and then return home for a late breakfast at 11:00 A.M.

I must have just missed meeting the three policemen who arrived at my brother's house minutes after I left. Quite oblivious of their visit, I returned to find that the happy home I had left was now a saddened shambles.

Security police had rudely awakened my brother's family at 4:00 demanding to search their

11

apartment—and search they did! Every drawer was pulled out, as were every cupboard, every box and file. They ransacked every available space, even searching through his books and the electric fuse box. My brother and his wife could only stand aside and watch the frenzied efforts, realizing that this was the beginning of a darkness without a dawn.

My brother was not the only victim. Other heartbroken pastors were hurriedly hustled away from their wives and families, and soon it became a case of "Who's next?" Waking up in the morning became an anxious experience of wondering if today was to be the last. Every knock on the door could be the final one. Every visitor might be the police. Fortunately, I was not married. I lived with my seventy-five-year-old father, my mother having died some years before.

One Sunday I preached a sermon in my church, taking as my text the words of Jesus: "Father, the hour is come; glorify thy Son, that thy Son may glorify thee." Christ had spoken these words knowing that He was soon to suffer for the world. How apt that message was. I too was about to suffer.

The hour had come; my agonized waiting was over; the next day I was arrested.

That morning of Monday, August 18, 1948 will never be erased from my memory. I awoke to the sound of sparrows arguing with each other in the guttering. It was warm and sunny, just perfect for fulfilling my promise to do some shopping for an elderly couple who lived on the opposite side of Russe.

I finished my visit toward the end of the morning and headed toward home feeling blissfully content after our fellowship together. As I turned the bend in the road, the warmth drained out of me when I saw four tall figures standing outside of my cottage. From where I stood, unseen

12

around the corner, I could clearly make out the men at the front door of our cottage; two were in police uniform, the other two in plain clothes. I felt my heart beating wildly, and a sense of panic rose within me. As I stood watching, two of them went inside. They certainly had not seen me and were obviously uncertain as to when I would arrive home. I guessed that there would be several hours to spare before they became suspicious of my whereabouts. This was to my advantage for it would give me plenty of time to travel many miles away from Russe, maybe even across the Bulgarian border. Yes, this seemed to be the obvious solution. Yet I stood watching, slightly uncertain as to what I should really do. Maybe they were searching for ammunition—as if they would find that in a church house!

At that moment my father emerged from the front door. He looked old, older than what he really was—maybe he was frightened. Again I became aware of the loud pounding of my heart beneath my jacket. What should I do? If I ran away and escaped across the border the authorities were sure to decree that this was obvious evidence of my guilt. Perhaps this would cause my congregation to disown me; and how would the young Christians respond to the behavior of their pastor? Then there was my dear father; what would become of him if I ran away? Suddenly, the answer became obvious: escaping would mean nothing; in fact, it would be miserable failure on my part.

I stood at the corner looking at the little cottage that I loved, all the time praying, "Lord, please help me! You know the truth. You know that there is nothing they can accuse me of. You know that I am not a spy."

And I walked deliberately down the road toward my home.

"What is your name?" was the curt question of

one of the policemen as I turned in at the front door of the cottage.

"Ladin Popov," I replied.

"Are you the pastor of the Evangelical Church in town?"

"Yes, I am."

"We have a warrant for your arrest. Get into some old clothes quickly and come with me."

With a calmness that surprised me, I asked, "Who has issued this warrant for my arrest, and kindly tell me what I am guilty of?"

"It's none of your business to know that," he snapped back at me, and pulling out a pistol, he pointed it at my chest. "Raise your hands, and get back into the house."

As I entered hands raised, it was evident that they had been searching everywhere. Clothing, papers, and books were scattered all over the floor and my dear old father was sobbing quietly in one corner of the room.

I changed as quickly as possible into some rather thin summer clothes—how I was later to regret that, because at the time the weather was warm and my panic-stricken mind was in no state to anticipate future possibilities. I was ready to go.

My father, still sobbing, moved from the corner shadows of the room to say good-by. He extended his thin arms to embrace and kiss me but one of the policemen, cursing loudly, stepped between us and roughly pushed him away. My father stumbled and crashed to the floor. This was to be my last sight of him, a pathetic, crumpled-up old man weeping his heart out for what was now to be two sons who faced communist persecution.

Unaware of what lay ahead for me, except for the assurance that God would always be with me, I was forcibly marched from my beloved home.

Our first stop was the bleak-looking District Office of the Ministry of Interior in the center of Russe. I knew the building very well from the outside, having passed by it numerous times during my many pastoral visits. Never in a hundred years would I have imagined myself locked behind its walls.

I was their latest prisoner, and prisoners are rarely treated politely or gently. They quickly searched me but what did they expect to find? Was it weapons they were after? It all seemed so crazy and senseless. Their attitude was one of acute suspicion and I sensed that if no justifiable accusation could be found, they would not hesitate in making one up.

After I was searched, I was directed down into what appeared to be a deep subterranean dungeon. Opening a door, they pushed me into a small dirty cell and left immediately, carefully locking the door behind them. Being underground, the cell had no windows. Illumination consisted of a single electric light bulb burning continuously in one corner. This was most disconcerting for I became completely oblivious to time. I had little idea of how long I was down there and this caused my mind to create depressing pictures of the suffering that I might have to face. Apparently, I remained in this frame of mind only a matter of hours. Early in the evening they returned, took me upstairs, out of the building, and across the town to the main police station where I was made to wait until 6:00. Under armed escort I boarded an awaiting train about fifteen minutes later, and we steamed slowly out of Russe bound for almost anywhere, for no one would tell me of our destination.

Mile after mile the train raced on through delightful countryside. Bulgaria is a beautiful land, and it was summer, which meant that evenings were much longer.

Some young people were singing at the far end of the coach. They could not have known how the words they sang stung my heart. "Good-by city, good-by city, we shall never see you again." This popular Bulgarian song brought tears to my eyes. How glad I was that they were too far away to notice.

I discovered later that the train was traveling roughly south, for two hours after leaving Russe we arrived at the large town of Gorna Orjahovitsa. Evidently there was no train to take me further that night for I was ordered to sleep at a police station in the town. There are many things that Communists cannot make you do merely by word of command; sleep is one of them. It was a very restless night, but I knew that the Lord was there with me.

In the morning several policemen arrived on duty at the station and among them, to my great surprise, was a friend named Ivan Dimitrov, whom I had not seen for a long time. Ivan was a Christian; in fact, he had been baptized and filled with the Holy Spirit in my own home. We had enjoyed enchanting times of fellowship together when he lived in Russe but eventually his work had moved him to a different station. But here I was looking into Ivan's warm brown eyes. After the strain of the last twenty-four hours, seeing a face that I knew was an immense comfort to me.

Quietly he asked me what I was doing here. I could not answer that; neither his second question as to what I had done. "Nothing!" I sobbed, and knowing me, he believed my reply.

After a number of questions to the authorities he gleaned a little information—information that appeared to worry him. Somehow he managed to arrange to be one of the men escorting me to Sofia. Yes, that was where I was going, to the Central Prison, Department A, of our capital city. Although I was ignorant of the significance of Department A, Ivan fully understood.

I recalled that when in Russe Ivan had often playfully said, "Brother Ladin, if anyone tries to harm you, I will help you." In my real moment of need there would be little that he could do to help.

We boarded the 8:00 train that took us about thirty-five miles west to the town of Levski where we stopped to refuel. Ivan was detailed only to escort me another twenty-five miles to Pleven, so if anything decisive was to happen, then this ten minutes' stop at Levski was the opportune moment. Gently taking me by the arm Ivan directed me into the station bathroom where he quietly explained about Department A.

"You must not go to Sofia, brother Ladin," he insisted. "Department A is dreadful. Come with me right now and we will escape to the mountains."

I was staggered by his offer of self-sacrifice. He was risking his life as well as his job. He really cared about me.

"But Ivan, I cannot escape," I replied. "I am amazed and grateful to think that you are prepared to risk everything for me but I will not let you. The Lord must surely have something planned in everything that is happening to me."

He put his arms around me and hugged me, pleading with me to change my mind, but in all conscience I could not do so.

"But you do not realize how appalling this place is where you are going," cried Ivan, raising his voice.

It was no act of heroism on my part that kept me from changing my mind. Quickly I tried to explain to Ivan knowing how brief time was, but he was not convinced. Ivan left me at Pleven and a new set of guards conducted me to Sofia.

Chapter Two

DEPARTMENT A: STATE SECURITY

I guess there are moments when everyone, the blessed saints included, flounders in excruciating patches of self-pity. I was no exception. I felt the whole world had turned its back on me, and even God had forgotten that I existed. But my thoughts also swung toward my dear brother Haralan and the other pastors whom we had heard were "missing." I began to draw comfort from the fact that they would understand how I was feeling right now.

I had no idea at the time as our train trundled along through sleepy summer fields that I was drawing nearer and nearer to my brother and many other pastors who had been so callously snatched away from wives and families.

The train crawled into Sofia at about 5:00 in the afternoon. Clearly my arrival had been meticulously planned; a Jeep was waiting to take me to the tall white building known as the headquarters of the Secret Police. How ironic that it should be painted white! Foreign visitors to Sofia would undoubtedly be impressed by it—that clean, efficient appearance of Secret Police heroically purging out corruption. But the local inhabitants knew better! They related stories of screams that pierced its walls and of many respected men who entered its doors never to come out again. Sofia's inhabitants knew only too well that the specialized, clean, white look was only surface paint.

Unknown to me at the time, not very far away, there were other imprisoned pastors. For most of us, each other's existence in the same forbidding building was to remain strictly secret. However, I did learn later that State Police authorities had been arresting Evangelical pastors since May of that year. I was one of the last to arrive.

The Secret Police wasted no time in making clear to me that they wanted information and they wanted it fast—information that I was sure would be twisted into some prefabricated tale and hurled back at me in court! They supplied me with pen and paper and ordered me to divulge the facts. But I was confused as to what I should write. Surely they did not want my entire life story? Yes, they insisted that they did. So I set about jotting down details of my life history, a description of the poverty that had been my childhood environment, about leaving school at fifteen and my first job in Sofia.

I could hardly help but tell them of how the Lord had reached down and saved me from a life of uselessness. I also wrote of my college days in Germany and England, and as much as I could remember about being a pastor.

After writing my first account they demanded even more details. So I rewrote my life story, racking my aching brain for the little incidents that had slipped my memory at the first. After handing them my second attempt they ordered me to write it yet again, then again and again! I could not understand this. Did they imagine that I was making it all up and by requesting me to rewrite I would make the fatal mistake of contradicting myself? I could hardly do that for it was an honest description of my life. I had nothing to hide.

By the time they informed me that I had written enough, an entire week had passed by. On reflection, I must have written volumes. It had been mentally exhausting but not entirely without its pleasant little moments when I was quietly able to praise the Lord as I recalled His gracious dealings in my life. My interrogators however were by no means satisfied.

Over the next few months I was to get to know the chief of Department A far better than what I would have normally wished to. His name was Georgy Tassev, a short, thick-set man with dark, piercing eyes. I was to learn the visible language of this man's words, gestures, and facial expressions that sprang from a cruel mind intent on doing its job oblivious of the suffering caused. I knew Jesus loved Georgy Tassev, but I found it hard to.

Tassev's strategy was to bludgeon me with sharp questions and subtle insinuations, until I wearied and gave up fighting for what I knew to be the truth. He so arranged things that every two hours one tired interrogator was replaced by a fresh one. I must have met dozens of Tassev's men, getting to know their mannerisms, as they got to know mine.

"When, where, and to whom did you supply information about the political and military life of this country?"

I replied that I had never belonged to any political organization. My answer failed to satisfy them.

I told them (as I had written in my "Police Station autobiography") about my childhood days when I worked on neighboring farms to earn that extra money that we so drastically needed, for our own little plot of ground scarcely supported our family. This was the sum total of my knowledge of Bulgarian economics.

As for my knowledge of military matters, I had never been in a responsible enough position to have known anything worth passing on to foreign powers. In fact, I did not even finish my military services. A few months before the date of my official discharge, I contracted pneumonia and was rushed to the military hospital dangerously ill. So what did I know of military secrets? I explained all this to my interrogators, but they were not convinced. I spent my military service more than ten years before the Communists took power in Bulgaria.

"When, where, and to whom did you give classified information?" This same question was hurled at me day and night, over and over again.

They knew, of course, that the churches in Bulgaria had links with Christian organizations in the West, but most of the comings and goings of Christian leaders and the helpful financial aid that the Western church gave to us was abandoned in 1944 when the Communists took over. Surely there had been no crime in this? But their repreated questioning began to make me wonder. Perhaps I had acted in some unethical way. Maybe I was guilty of crimes against the state. It was in discouraging moments as this that the Lord would gently come and reassure me of my innocence.

Then they commenced starving me. I was given a nearly tasteless liquid that could hardly have been anything more than the water left over after boiling beans. This insipid bean broth sometimes had a faint hint of tomatoes, paprika, and onions, but it could in no way be described as nourishing. The miserable mixture was served in portions that would fill five spoons. My daily diet consisted of five spoonfuls at midday and five spoonfuls in the evening with two slices of dry bread on each occasion.

Thank God, since becoming a pastor in 1939, I had never been short of good food. The dear people that I shepherded had given generously to me even to the point of sometimes denying themselves of basic human needs.

Having sufficient food had not always been a regular feature of my life. There were times when our family drifted near starvation. Once, when I was nearly two years old, the family had sat down to a Christmas dinner of only onions and dried peppers cooked and dipped in vinegar. My dear father was away from home on military service at that time and although the local authorities were responsible for handing out portions of corn meal, these were by no means sufficient or regular. We were a poor family. I had grown up in the absence of luxuries, but we did have each other. Now I was alone and this starvation diet was almost the limit. I felt that I was slowly being driven into a pit of black despair. The authorities clearly intended to keep me alive, but just about! They undoubtedly anticipated that a lack of nourishment would numb my mind into believing and saying anything.

For nearly a month they wore me down with a meager diet and endless questioning but even through all of this my suffering was not entirely without its reward. The Bible contains a letter penned by the apostle Paul, one that never would have been written if it had not been for Paul's "chance" meeting with a fellow prisoner—a slave by the name of Onesimus. The charming little letter reveals how Onesimus was wonderfully converted to Christ in that depressing prison cell and how he humbly returned to his master from whom he had run away.

No runaway slaves turned up in my cell but the Lord certainly directed an interesting variety of people whom I was able to help.

Chapter Three

A BOY CALLED OGNIAN

Whatever went on in the outside world of Bulgaria's busy capital city, it rarely affected the noisy internal activity of the Secret Service building where I was at present imprisoned. But for once it was relatively quiet, much of the movement of the police officers being hushed by their soft-soled shoes. This peace was suddenly shattered as my cell door crashed open and a young man was roughly pushed inside. This iron door with its tiny peephole clanged shut, and there we were, two of us cramped together in Cell 15. For a few moments there was a stony silence. The sullen looking young man with matted hair and tattered clothes stared at me briefly and then flung himself down in a corner, acting as though he was the sole occupier of this depressing prison box. His frightened eyes began darting over every bleak inch of our cell walls—they stared at me and quickly turned away as if to say, "You are an enemy, and I would rather you were not here."

In an attempt to lead him into conversation, I softly said, "Where are you from my friend?" He said nothing. Rather apologetically, I spoke again. "You seem rather upset. Won't you tell me why you were arrested?" He continued to remain silent and I realized that pumping questions at him was obviously the wrong line of approach.

I was concerned about him but at the same

time felt rather frustrated about being unable to reach him. I tried again.

"Try to calm yourself; don't you realize that life is made up of both happy days and sad days, and we must use the strength inside us to confront both? Please tell me about yourself."

He merely glanced back at me with eyes full of antagonism.

"Have they tortured you so much that you cannot speak, my friend?" I asked. "You have no reason to fear me; I am a prisoner just like yourself."

But as much as I tried to communicate; he remained reticent to talk. He was treating me as if he hated me—why should he do this? Maybe he thought I was an informer placed in Cell 15 for the sole reason of finding out what I could about him and then submitting a report to the authorities. It was certainly obvious that he did not want me disturbing his thoughts, so I left him alone.

I sat down in a corner and our silence was broken only by his nervous, heavy breathing.

Suddenly, without any warning he leaped to his feet, strode across the few feet of our tiny cell and began hammering his head against the whitewashed wall. For a moment I was shocked to immobility as over and over and over again he battered his skull into the hard stone, screaming, "I want to die! I want to die! I can't take any more torture. What have I done to deserve this? Why do they want to destroy me?"

After what seemed ages, I grabbed him, struggling to pull him away from the blood-smeared wall.

"Stop this and don't be a fool," I shouted. "You'll kill yourself if you continue doing this. If the guards hear you they will punish you even more than what you are punishing yourself."

He tried to free himself from my grasp, and we both lost our balance and tumbled into a heap on the floor. Our eyes met. It seemed as though some of that anger and hatred had ebbed away. Hopefully, he was beginning to realize that my concern for him was sincere.

"Who are you, and where are you from?" he gasped.

"I am Ladin Popov from Russe, imprisoned in connection with the pastors' case," I replied.

"And I thought you were a communist spy," he said with much more trust in his voice. "Please forgive me."

The ice was broken; we began to talk.

I soon discovered that he was quite an influential young man. Toward the end of the war he had become a lieutenant in the First Bulgarian Division that had fought against the Germans in Yugoslavia and Hungary, and for leadership and gallantry he had been acclaimed a hero. After the war he became active against suppression, and up until the day of his arrest, an organizer in the youth opposition group known as N. Petkov. During the recent Bulgarian elections he was one among many who had been responsible for numerous activities planned to make life, to say the least, uncomfortable for the Communists. Members of his organization had been meticulously watched by the police and then arrested one by one. The authorities had firm intentions of leaving no one around capable of any acts of subversion.

"They will destroy us all," he sighed wearily, his whole attitude revealing the utter hopelessness of the situation.

I understood the pointlessness of his stuggle, but at the same time I refused to share it. Here I was in the same cell awaiting a possible fate as dismal as his, but I knew that the ministry to which I had been called was divinely directed.

The Lord was beginning to show me that the physical obstacles of walls, pain, an even fear, were not barriers to the glory of His presence. In fact, my soul was beginning to burn for a divine cause that I knew had guided me here. But what existed for this young man? His campaign was finished, his life was in jeopardy, and the future held nothing.

I blinked my eyes; he was speaking to me again, and this time more peacefully. "I am from Chervena Voda, Russenko. I used to live in Russe; in fact, quite near to your Protestant church, and although I cannot call myself a practicing believer I am certainly not an atheist. My name is Ognian Christov Nedelchev."

I liked him and longed to share with him my increased awareness of the presence of Jesus.

"Listen, Ognian," I said, "you can be sure that you will not be destroyed by the Communists. You'll leave here well and healthy to enjoy blissful freedom again. But please don't hurt yourself anymore. Let me have a look at your head for it must be swollen."

He stepped meekly over to me and I began examining the grazing and swellings.

"I cannot let you kill yourself, Ognian," I said, parting his matted hair while inspecting the ugly swellings. "I want to tell you that God loves you dearly. He longs for you to be His child. This is the reason why Jesus died on the cross, that you might realize what forgiveness is all about. He died for you."

Frankly, Ognian's sudden response shook me. I had hardly finished speaking when he fell to his knees on the floor crying, "God, please forgive me; I know that I have sinned against You, but I want Jesus to forgive me."

During my pastoral ministry I have heard many people pray words similar to these, but never so quickly in response to what I had said. This must surely have been the Holy Spirit gently prodding him into submission. My heart was thrilled to overflowing.

Just a short time before Ognian had been antagonistic toward me, but in a matter of minutes the Holy Spirit had rushed into the turmoil of his life bringing an incredible sense of peace and forgiveness.

The presence of the Lord seemed to fill the cramped emptiness of that tiny prison cell as we praised and thanked Him together. Ognian seemed so overpowered with love and gratitude to God that like a little child he literally leaped up and down with joy. He threw his arms around me, hugging and thanking me again and again for speaking to him about the Lord.

There was a great need for Ognian to learn, and I was delighted that I had nothing else to do but teach him. For several days we revelled in our newfound Christian fellowship together until one morning, quite unexpectedly, he was snatched away from Cell 15 as quickly as he had been thrown in. I never saw Ognian again.

Chapter Four

THE TORTURE COMMENCES

Days shuffled slowly by. I eventually discovered that I had been in Cell 15 for three weeks. The date was now September 9, a national holiday celebrating the communist takeover four years before.

Through the tiny window of my cell wafted the exciting sounds and spicy smells of holiday activities in the streets far below. I certainly wasn't enthusiastic about joining in communist celebrations, but the aroma of the food cooking right beneath my window jolted my attention onto the frequent hunger pains that had begun wrenching my body. The noisy bustle of holiday crowds, and the appetizing fragrance of barbecued pork chops magnified the depressing conditions of my imprisonment beyond all proportion.

Somewhere, however, mingling among the surging festive crowds were a handful of daring young men with armfuls of anti-communist posters. One was caught by the Secret Police as he was hurriedly pasting his illegal posters on a shop wall. Information was quickly extracted and later that day the entire group was arrested. One of the victims, a poorly dressed, tall young man, was thrown into my cell. It was quite obvious that he had been through rough treatment since the moment of his arrest. He squatted in a corner, stared nervously at me for a while and then looked away.

Presuming that he was too frightened to

speak, I opened the conversation. "Where are you from, friend, and why were you brought here?"

"I live on Washington Street, in Sofia," he replied cautiously. "My mother is a seamstress; my father died when I was quite young." With that he began quietly sobbing. "I am her only son and I do not know how she is going to cope with me in here. I do love her, and I know she loves me." He buried his face in his hands, shaking and weeping uncontrollably.

"Don't cry," I murmured, "let me tell you about Someone who has been through what you and your mother are going through. He can help you more than what you can ever imagine."

I tried not to speak above a whisper, being acutely aware of how much the Communists hated the indoctrination of children and young people. The possibility existed that they had placed the young man in my cell in order to find out what I would do and say. Maybe they had already heard about my conversation with Ognian.

"Who is it then who can comfort my mother?" asked the faltering voice from the far corner of the cell.

"Jesus Christ," I whispered. "Do you believe in Him?" I asked this as gently as I could.

He appeared confused as to what to say. Understandably, he did not know who I was, and he had probably heard of what the Secret Police do with young Christians in prison.

I suspected that the troubled eyes that stared back at me were saying, "I believe, I believe!" He was all but mouthing the words, but a lurking fear checked him.

"Please do not be afraid of me," I pleaded. "I am a Protestant pastor and I can appreciate that you do not want your feelings to be known in case the atheists find out."

My comment appeared to help considerably.

The troubled look vanished from his face as he realized that the authorities would not be informed of our conversation.

"My mother has a beautiful icon," he remarked eagerly. "Every evening before going to bed she lights a candle and whispers her prayers. The icon is a picture of the crucifixion of Jesus."

"So you know something about Him," I interjected.

"Yes, but I must tell you, comrade, that from a little child, right through school, we were taught that there is no God. If a student as much as hinted of the existence of God, he was either thrown out or put down a grade or two. If we openly confessed to believing in God, it would mean immediate closed doors to our careers. All our students were taught to persecute Christian believers.

"I am not a Communist—I hate them, but I have had to go along with them in order to construct some sort of future for myself."

"Why do you think your mother prays?" I said in order to swing our conversation around on a more personal basis.

"I'm not against praying," he replied. "I believe that there is a supernatural power in the universe but no one knows who or what it is."

"There I must disagree with you," I answered. "There are people who personally know this Power, a Power that openly reveals itself to all who cry out for help. This Power, the One in which your dear mother finds comfort, is God. He sent His Son, Jesus, from heaven to live in our lives. Jesus Christ is the manifestation of that Power."

Suddenly a loud crash in the outside corridor interrupted us. The cell door lurched open and three guards strode in. For a matter of seconds they gazed around in angry silence and then left as abruptly as they had come. I looked at the young man opposite me; he was shaking with fear. Since he did not understand the reason for the guards' behavior, I explained that this was a part of their plan in unnerving prisoners. Because they wanted quick confessions out of us, even of crimes we had never committed, the breaking-down strategy of shock visits was adopted.

From the guards' action, I suspected that we were being watched so I did not pursue our line of conversation. We remained silent listening to faraway sounds from the world beyond and the faint drone of human voices behind the thick cell walls of the world within.

After a while, however, I whispered, "Why are you here?"

"It all happened yesterday," he said in hushed response. "We pasted up anti-communist posters in the city."

"What sort of things did the posters say?" I asked, quite intrigued.

"Some read, 'Cursed be the shameful date of the taking over of our free people by the Communists!' Others read, 'We want our freedom from the Communists!' We fastened them onto lampposts and walls; in fact, anywhere we could. Unfortunately one of us was caught and forced to divulge all our names."

I was quietly contemplating the dedication of these young men when his raised voice summoned my attention.

"I'm so hungry! My mother, you know, makes delicious pancakes; we have them every morning."

I gently assured him that he would have to get used to being hungry. Every prisoner was treated like we were.

In spite of the fact that we had done little else but talk, we both began to feel very drowsy. Looking round our scant cell, my young friend commented, "Is this the way you sleep in here, on the floor without bed or covering? Don't they at least supply the prisoners with mats?"

"No," I answered, "we sleep on the floor, but, thank God, the floor is at least a wooden one rather than cold cement. Compared with the plight of many prisoners, we are fortunate. Always remember that we have been brought here to be destroyed, not pampered."

Reluctantly the boy curled up in one corner of the cell, and I in the other; the boards were hard but eventually sleep came.

My next sensation was that of being dragged out of sleep by a loud pounding on our cell door. It was my companion, fists clenched, beads of sweat on his forehead and doubled up with what was obviously severe stomach pains. He muttered about having had mild appendix trouble over the past few weeks.

I commenced thumping on the door in an effort to attract someone's attention and, after what seemed ages, it eventually swung open. I recognized the policeman blocking the doorway, and quickly explained the situation to him. "Comrade, this young boy is ill. He has severe pains in his side resulting from a history of appendicitis. Can you help him?"

"No one asked him to come here," was the angry, pitiless response. "Let him die. People like him should die anyway." He slammed the door and the sound of his footsteps faded into the semi-darkness.

The night dragged slowly on as did his stomach pains, becoming worse rather than better. All I could do was place my arm around his shoulders and pray.

"Comrade, I'm dying," he moaned. "The pain is unbearable. Oh, my poor mother, I'll never see her again. God help me for no one else can."

At that moment our cell door opened again, and in walked a doctor with two security agents. He quickly diagnosed a ruptured appendix and ordered him to be rushed to the hospital.

I was alone again, but the Lord had heard our prayers. I only hope that the young man recognized this.

I knew that I was in Cell 15 of Department A, Central Security, for a reason, a part of that reason being the opportunities I was receiving in witnessing to my fellow cell mates. But I sensed that there was a great deal more to my being here that I did not yet know about. It is the mind of the Almighty to compassionately hide the future from us. If I had known in the beginning what I had to face, I would undoubtedly have gone insane. His plan was certainly for me to go from strength to strength, even though physically I was becoming considerably weaker.

One afternoon I was escorted from my cell for what I guessed would be a session of further questioning. My interrogator was a handsome curly-haired man whom I had not met before. His questioning began with the usual "What, where and whom?" repeated in rapid staccato fashion. I dutifully gave him correct, honest answers that seemed to enrage, rather than appease.

After what must have been forty-five minutes at the same tiresome game, he suddenly dragged open a small drawer in his desk and snatched out a little book that I immediately recognized as a New Testament. He flicked it open to the title page, thrust it in front of my face and yelled, "Where was this produced?"

"Printed in the U.S.A.," I replied composedly, for it clearly signified this at the bottom of the page.

Snapping it shut, he hit me in the face with it before I had time to brace myself.

"Yes," he snarled, "the U.S.A. All your life you have preached pro-Americanism in our country, and still you pretend that you never delivered any information. Who do you think you are lying to? To yourself? To God? To us Communists?"

"It is not my wish to lie to anyone, Comrade Superior," I replied as calmly as I was able. "Up to this present moment I have told you nothing but the truth."

Again he slapped me across the face. "So you still continue to remain obstinate? But we'll see how long it is before you change your mind," and he pushed me out of the room, screaming, "When you've learned what suffering is, things will be different."

With obvious frustration at my lack of cooperation, he ordered that I be taken to the chief interrogator, Georgy Tassev.

Tassev was not alone in his room. As I entered, a tall young man confronted me, introducing himself as Ljubcho, personal assistant to Comrade Georgy Tassev.

"You are going to plead guilty, aren't you?" he said in a soft voice.

"Guilty of what?" I replied.

"Of what we tell you," decreed Ljubcho staring straight across the room at me.

"I will certainly listen. Please tell me."

In the icy silence that followed, Ljubcho glanced hurriedly at his superior and then walked across the room to face me.

"Listen, Ladin, it is for your good. Don't be so stubborn. All you have to do is plead guilty. I can tell you that when a man pleads guilty we do not punish him. We are all human and we all make mistakes. You have been influenced by older men and, being younger, you have been deceived by them. All we want you to do is to acknowledge this. It is all for your good."

As I listened to the warm pleading of his soupy voice, it all seemed so clear—so obviously right. They were being friendly, and it was friendly voices that I desperately needed to hear. Maybe it was the only sensible thing to do even if their pleas were not true. I looked at Ljubcho as he waited, and

34

suddenly I caught Tassev's hungry glare that immediately jolted me back to reality.

"Can a man confess things that he has never done?" I asked Ljubcho politely.

This angered Tassev. Holding out his hands like the pans of a weighing scales, he said, "Now listen to me, Ladin. Here is your life, and this is your death. Which are you going to choose?"

"That's an easy choice," I replied. "I want life, of course."

"All right, then" Tassev continued, "all you have to do is to write down the things we tell you. Over there is the door; do as you are told and you will go out free—no one will stop you. If you refuse my requests—here is death," he explained, raising his hand and clenching it tightly into a fist until his fingers turned white.

"But, Mr. Tassev, how shall I write things I know nothing about? I just haven't the information that you require." It was at this moment that their acting suddenly ceased. Soft, oily words and carefully reasoned arguments became streams of venomous anger. With curses and foul language they began to threaten me with all manner of horrifying punishments.

Tassev ordered his assistant to get something, the name of which I did not understand. Ljubcho scurried away returning a few minutes later holding what appeared to be a set of handcuffs. Forcing my hands behind my back, he snapped them on. The pain that accompanied their closing told me that they were not the normal handcuffs that I had been used to. The slightest movement pierced my wrists with excruciating pains. I learned afterward that these steel bands had thirty sharp needles that pointed inward.

Tassev looked at me as I winced with the pain. "From today we regard you as our number one enemy. Now get out!"

The steel jaws bit deeper as gaurds hauled me

by one arm out of Tassev's office. An intelligence officer conducted me back to my cell and ordered me to remain standing perfectly still; otherwise, he warned, the guards would beat the instructions home with wooden batons.

So wearily I stood still in my desolate cell and, in spite of the nagging pain, was able to lift my heart to the Lord and thank Him for preserving me so far and for giving me the courage to face the communist authorities. There were even moments when my pain seemed to ease as I talked to the Lord and sang Christian songs. Although forbidding me to sit down they had said nothing about singing.

I was not alone in the cell; there was another prisoner, a man from the city of Sofia. He had only recently been arrested, having been brought from State Security's Department Number Fifteen. He was rather agitated, and turned very pale when he saw the type of handcuffs pinned to my wrists, but as the hours dragged wearily on, he became increasingly eager to help releive me of the pain that I was suffering. It became necessary for him to feed me and assist in other ways; in fact, we learned quite a few tricks as my agony intensified. He would periodically massage my neck and shoulders, and by lying on the floor with his legs stretched straight out, I was able to lean my chest on his feet and thus ease much of the weight from my legs.

With my arms being constantly held down the blood in my veins was not finding its way back into general circulation; this resulted in my arms beginning to swell. It was a vicious circle, for the more they became bloated with blood, the deeper the teeth of the handcuffs bit into them. Blood trickled from the gashes and dried on my shin, and later, as my arms swelled even more, I began to hear the blood dripping onto the floor behind me. Hour after hour I was compelled to stand as if nailed to the floorboards.

My cell companion felt great pity for me, but really, there was little he could do to relieve my pain. In an effort to distract myself from my suffering, and also because my friend appeared to be an eager listener, I began to talk to him about the Lord. In fact, we talked on and on into the night and I shared with him the loving claims of Jesus Christ on our lives. Although insisting that he was an atheist, he nevertheless seemed impressed at the courage and faith that I was apparently showing during my sufferings.

"I don't believe in God," he admitted candidly, "but your courage in the face of this harsh punishment deeply moves me. There must be some Power that supports you and conveys the calmness to act so bravely."

"I was scared," he said, "when I saw you with those monstrous handcuffs on, but your words of comfort deeply moved me. You gave me courage when, by rights, I should have been giving it to you."

Saturday night passed, and I continued to stand all through Sunday. By then the feeling in my arms had completely gone; I did not even feel the stabs of the handcuffs.

When I was not talking to my cell mate, I was finding great comfort in prayer. It neither released me from prison, nor changed my circumstances, but somehow I was able to accept things more graciously, including the pain.

I often prayed for the guards and interrogators, sometimes in their presence. As they tortured me, I insisted in my prayers, even though frequently they were nothing but reminders to myself that if ever these people should be in the same situation that I was in, with their lives threatened and their bodies in pain, I would help them survive.

The next day, Monday, at about 10:00 a high-ranking official entered my cell. He seemed horrified to see the condition that I was in, still standing of course, with my arms swollen and a pool of dried blood at my feet. He hurried away to find Tassev and obtain a key to unlock my manacles, but Tassev couldn't be found; apparently, he was taking a day off hunting in the mountains. With mild amusement I wondered whether he was so annoyed at being unable to get information out of me that he had decided to indulge his annoyance on wolves, bears, and boars?

After an unsuccessful search for the keys a police official found a pair of metal cutting pincers and snipped the steel handcuffs from my wrists. The pain was agonizing, but the relief of having my hands free more than compensated. Even I was shocked to see the mess that the handcuffs had made of my wrists.

For four or five hours my arms remained completely numb. It felt as though they did not belong to me, but as feeling gradually returned it helped counterbalance the growing discomfort of having to forcibly remain standing.

The same day that my handcuffs were cut off my cell companion was released. I was alone again.

Days dragged by as endlessly as the nights. I felt that I was becoming like a statue in the middle of the cell floor. I even began to wonder if my body would ever remember how to walk again. I could feel the blood making my legs swell; they felt like lead but the guards still forced me to remain standing. I wasn't even allowed access to a wash basin to clean the dried blood from my fatigued limbs. Night and day for two whole weeks I stood with no rest or sleep, thoroughly unkempt, unshaven and filthy. My only comfort was a pleasant sense of the presence of God.

My interrogators continued relentlessly in their questioning. Time and time again I would be ordered from the cell to stumble, weak and ill, along the dismal winding corridors to the chief interrogator's room. Their ceaseless questionings drained me, and what for? It all seemed so utterly pointless and ridiculous, but they persisted in the subtle strategy of trying to trip me into contradicting myself, thereby making me a liar.

They even tried scaring me into telling lies, slapping me round the face and beating me up, but I was so tired I hardly felt the blows. Looking back now, it was wonderful how the Lord enabled me to remain in control of my mind throughout these ordeals. Although I must have lapsed into semi-consciousness on more than one occasion, nevertheless, I know that nothing proceeded from my lips that could honestly incriminate me in a court of law.

One evening I was bundled down some stairs into a depressing underground room where my captors began showing me various torture appliances for stretching human bodies and for slowly beating people to death. After torture, the unfortunate victims were plunged into concrete tubs full of icy water to remove traces of the beatings.

I was ordered to strip off my shirt as they directed me across to the other side of the room. In front of me stood a wooden cross. Unlike the cross of my Lord this one was riveted to the ground. It was constructed in such a way that when a person was tied to it, his arms and legs could be slowly stretched until sinews and joints were torn and the person lost consciousness in a haze of agony. Those who did not recover were dragged outside and buried in a nearby graveyard. For those who somehow remained alive after the primitive inquisitional stretching, one can only assume that they were deformed beyond imagination.

"Plead guilty now and you will be free," I was told as I stared around in horror. "If not, you will be stretched on the cross. Think it over; you have two minutes."

So this was the end. My stomach heaved in

sickness and dread. All I could do was to quickly pray a silent prayer. "O God, if You permit my being subjected to the torture of this cross, please give me the strength to put up with the pain. Please come to my rescue, please!"

To my rescue He immediately came, for I suddenly felt the warm comforting light of His presence shaft into my stricken mind. All my aches and pains as well as my fearful thoughts seemed to wash away as His love gushed into me. *Somehow I felt quite prepared for the torture of the cross and even for death.* Maybe this was how those early Christians felt as they huddled together in the amphitheater waiting to be set upon by starved, wild beasts.

The interrogators, probably thinking that this time they would wring out the answers they wanted, again began grilling me with the same old questions. Like a record played over and over again, I heard myself repeating in a faraway voice, "Never, to no one, nowhere." There was silence, and for some minutes I awaited their response in a sort of daze.

"Put your shirt on and get back to your cell," snarled one of the policemen.

I could hardly believe the words that I heard and wept in gratitude to the heavenly Father who had heard my prayer sobbed from deep underground and had prevented the horrific torture promised by my persecutors.

For two long weeks I had been standing without a break. This and the starvation diet of little more than bread and water had reduced me to utter weakness. It had been three months since I had eaten anything that could be regarded as substantial and I had now become so drained and exhausted that a little child could have pushed me over. At last my guards allowed me to sleep, but the meager diet continued.

This relaxation of torture lasted just one week.

Once more I was ordered to stand continuously. Interrogation continued, directed each time by a new face. My one week's break from standing had been insufficient to refresh me. I needed much more sleep.

This time I found that I was unable to remain standing. The nights were the hardest to endure; my body refused to tolerate the sleeplessness and fatigue and I began falling to the floor and losing consciousness. Outside of my cell the patrolling guard, hearing me fall, would rush in, beat me into consciousness, and thrust me back on my feet again. Soon I would faint and fall down yet again and the guard would once more kick me into consciousness and heave me up to my feet. This terrible torment went on for twenty-one days, twenty-four hours a day.

I remember that toward the end my mind was so shattered I could not remember words said to me even over short periods. I began hallucinating; the scratches on the walls writhed into people rushing toward me in huge black crowds. The knots in the rough wooden floorboards became the learing faces of Stalin, Roosevelt, and Churchill. I was being slowly sucked into a black whirlpool of fatigue, and all I could do was to wearily lean in the arms of Christ recalling words from Scripture promising me that He would not let anyone be tempted beyond their strength. He also promised that there would be an avenue of escape in order that we might be able to endure. No escape was visible to me. Surely I was at my limit?

Unless you have sunk to the point where human endurance is held by the thinnest wisp of spider's web, it will be very hard for you to conceive what my suffering was like, just as it is difficult for me to describe it. I felt that I was living in a perpetual nightmare where the grotesque and hideous were at times more real than the natural and ordinary. The endless barrage of beatings and

41

questionings, the constant standings and fallings, seem almost unbelievable to me now.

Finally, and in what must have been an incoherent voice, I pleaded with the guard who kept watch on me, to conduct me to the inspector assigned to the trial of Evangelical pastors. His name was Mannov. As I was dragged along brightly lit passages to his office, my mind was too numb to register surprise that my request had actually been granted.

"Mr. Mannov," I mumbled in slow deliberation, "I have come to you to make the following proposition. If in all your examination you have found the remotest evidence that during my activities as a pastor I acted as a spy, then I will sign a declaration and you can take out your pistol and shoot me. If, however, you want to kill me because of my faith in God, you may do this also; I am ready to die. For either of these, I am ready to sign a declaration right now.

"If the inquiry has not proved that I acted as a spy, and if you do not wish to kill me because of my belief in God, then I beg you to call off these terrible punishments. My strength cannot hold out much longer, and my body is black and blue with bruises from repeatedly falling to the floor. I tell you, I would gladly embrace death rather than face more torture. Please stop this terrible treatment because I know I am not guilty."

My weary mind had drawn upon its last ounce of strength to make this plea. Mr. Mannov had listened patiently without once interrupting and contradicting me. He asked no questions and, in my fuzzy brain, there leaped a spark of hope. Without taking his eyes off me, he called his assistant to him and whispered something in his ear. The agent took me by the arm and led me back to my cell, informing me that my punishment was called off.

The relief was overwhelming, and after three weeks of unmitigated horror, I slumped to the floor and instantly fell asleep, remaining there right through that day and night and the entire day that followed. It was on the third day that I climbed unsteadily to my feet again, feeling completely refreshed. The first thing I noticed after rubbing my eyes were the words scrawled on the upper side of the door frame. "Here only God can help you—God help those who suffer!" I had read it before, but now I praised God that I had seen its fulfillment.

It was on the 2nd of November that a large man was pushed roughly into my cell. He looked around him and nodded at me. Standing in the middle of our tiny room he began reading the writings that previous prisoners had scratched into the white staring walls. On reading "Here only God can help you," he stopped, sighed, and politely asked me if there were any chairs or beds to sit on.

"No, comrade," I replied. "All we have is what you see. You haven't visited this sort of place before, have you?"

Instead of answering my question, he quickly threw another one at me.

"Where do you sleep at night? Surely there must be blankets?"

"We sleep on the floor," I told him, "and we sleep with all our clothes on so as to keep warm."

"Why is it you are growing a beard?" he continued inquisitively. "Don't they allow you to shave either?"

I explained that not only were we forbidden to shave, but I had not been permitted to wash my face for three months.

Looking sadly around the cell, he sighed again as he realized the total lack of everyday amenities.

Desiring to get to know him more, I endeavored to reassure him that this was by no means the worst prison area to be in, and I suggested that he sit down on the floor so that he could talk more comfortably.

Being quite a heavy man, he found this rather awkward. I waited while he made himself as comfortable as was possible in such cramped conditions, and then asked him where he was from and why he had been arrested.

"I am from Sofia," he murmured dejectedly, "and a dentist by profession."

On inquiring about his arrest, he remarked that it was for an absolutely ridiculous reason.

"Last week a few of my friends and I were having a meal in a restaurant. I guess we must have had too much to drink. We were joking with each other and I even jested about trying to escape from Bulgaria through Greece. Among our groups was a major by the name of Lisichkov. He quickly reported me, and at noon today I was arrested. It was all a joke of course, but my comments have been taken seriously."

My dentist companion was interrogated for a number of days after which punishment began. Like myself, he was denied food and forced to remain standing indeterminately.

Just like any hungry man he began voicing his longings. "If only I could have just a small piece of cheese and a slice of fresh bread," was his plaintive cry one day.

Recalling the young man who craved for pancakes, I endeavored to make him understand that in a place like this food was a luxury. In fact, there would be some weeks when he would never even see a slice of dry bread. It was a case of being cruel to be kind. Grasping the stark reality of the situation would help counterbalance the nagging longings that had no hope of fulfillment. Because of his excess weight he would at least have a reserve that would assist him in enduring the hunger pangs for a few more days yet. I knew only too well how tormenting the thoughts of food can be in such conditions, and endeavored to do everything possible in directing our conversation around the subject.

It was now the beginning of a cold and wet November. At night as the gray rain ran down, the wind beating against the walls of our cell, I would imagine that the endless dripping water was a lonely mother shedding tears for her lost children. The lone owl that hooted mournfully in the dim distance would remind me of the many lamenting prisoners suffering through the long November nights.

"My feet are so sore," moaned my dentist companion painfully. "I'll sit down for a while—no one will see me."

"No, don't!" I whispered in sudden panic. "You are continually being watched through a peephole in the door. If they catch you sitting down your punishment will be worse."

I had hardly uttered my warning when there was a loud crash on our cell door. Obviously we had been seen. My friend jumped nervously to his feet whispering vehemently, "These Communists are animals; they haven't any decent, human feelings. Why are they making me stand night and day? What do they want from me?"

He swung around, grabbed me by the shoulders and hissed, "Listen, comrade, if you ever meet a Communist after this, kill him!"

Although he had spoken in a whisper, I urged him to refrain from speaking that way. The guards would need to hear only his whispers, and he would feel the intensified force of their anger. I told him of the appalling tortures inflicted on people who had dared to speak as he had spoken. I related some of my own experiences, including that of how I had been forced to stand for three weeks. He had difficulty believing me.

As had been done for me, I lay down on the floor with my legs stretched straight out so that he could lean his chest on my feet. "Bravo, Popov," he exclaimed with obvious relief, "this is a wonderful way to rest."

During the night of November 7 they took me from my cell, but not to freedom.

Chapter Five

THE VISION

It was now nearly four months since I had become a prisoner of the Secret Police, and during this time I had become accustomed to their terrifying treatment of human beings. Without this preparation, unpleasant as it was, I would have found the terrifying night of November 7 rather hard to believe.

The dentist and I were fast asleep in our cell when suddenly two agents burst in bellowing at us and kicking us into consciousness.

"You, man, what is your name?" yelled one, his boot crashing into my ribs and taking my breath away. "Come on, answer me quickly."

I gasped for air, wondering what punishment they had in mind this time.

"Ladin Popov," I replied as they repeatedly shouted their questions.

"Get up then, and be quick about it," they commanded.

It seemed as though it was only me that they wanted, but what for?

The dentist lay silent, quite flabbergasted by their bestial behavior.

I dragged myself to my feet, and at the instructions of one of the agents, scooped up my few belongings and followed them out of the cell.

We walked quickly through the winding corridors of the headquarters building passing the many small miserable cells where other "criminals" were endeavoring to sleep away the suffering from their memories. Eventually we made our exit out of a door at the rear of the building, and there in the courtyard was a jeep with its door already open for me to climb in.

So I was leaving State Security Building, but where to? Many had entered and not come out alive; I had, but clearly it was not to be released.

With guns pointing at me they ordered me to climb into the jeep. The doors were slammed and we screamed off down the darkened streets.

It was impossible to tell where we were going. I instinctively imagined the worst, that we were headed out of the city toward a quiet country lane where I would be shot in cold blood—the official explanation being "attempted escape." I knew that it had happened before with so-called "uncooperative" prisoners.

Naturally, I was scared, and in the cold November night I called out silently to God, "Lord, if it is Your will that my life be extinguished in this way, give me Your strength to lay down my life bravely and joyfully."

The jeep raced on through the dark, deserted streets until in the distance I perceived the glow of a well-lit structure that was obviously our destination. Two minutes later we swung into the main entrance of a forbidding looking building surrounded by high stone walls with ramparts. The jeep screeched to a standstill, and I was ordered out at pistol point and led toward a large iron gate that swung open with a morbid clang. It was then that I noticed the sign "Central Prison," and with a sigh of relief I realized that this was my present destination; it was not a bullet through the head in a silent country road. But on entering the vast government building even the thought of further imprisonment became rather daunting as I heard the unmistakable sounds of screaming, shouting, and crying.

I was directed to climb a tall stairway that led to the iron gateway entrance of Department 7. Two policemen opened the gate from the inside and I was shoved roughly along a long corridor lined on either side with solid metal doors with numbers on them. We halted at number 219, the door was opened, and I was pushed in. It was the intense cold and overpowering smell of mildew that immediately struck me as I stood there. Undoubtedly my cell was extremely damp.

As soon as the police left me, I began rummaging among my meager belongings for a small bar of perfumed soap that I knew was there. This would at least help disguise the smell of the mildew, but it was only by holding it close to my nose that the stifling odor diminished.

Some minutes later the cell door opened, and four plain wooden boards were thrown in. Experience told me that these were my bed. Laid on the floor side by side they were just wide enough for me to lie on. I was to be thankful for these bare boards, for the floor was solid concrete and judging by the cold air in my cell the floor would literally become icy as winter set in. I found out later that some prisoners had only newspapers for a bed, whereas my wooden boards provided much better insulation. It seems hard, looking back from a more comfortable way of life, to think of how grateful one could be for the simple fact of sleeping on boards instead of newspaper. I thankfully regarded it as a token of God's grace and love.

Before trying to get some sleep, I carefully surveyed my cell, immediately observing that the intense cold was partly caused by broken glass in the single window above my head. I also noticed that each of the four walls was splattered by the red-brown smudges of squashed bed bugs, the obvious victims of former prison occupants. Then, with nothing else to do, I wrapped myself as tightly as possible in the single thin blanket and lay down on the bed planks. But sleep was as far away as the ice of the stars. My cell was freezing and the musty stench of mildew suffocating. I got up and attempted to keep warm by wrapping myself tighter in the blanket. This failed, so I tried hugging myself and jumping up and down like a grasshopper in a jam jar, regretting again and again that I hadn't thought of wearing warmer clothes on the day of my arrest, instead of the silly light things that I had hurriedly slipped into. Conserving bodily heat in my spindly physique was a near impossibility.

It wasn't long before my exercises made me out of breath, so I set myself to reading some of the inscriptions scratched into the walls. There were the popular ones, "Only God can help you here," "God help the sufferer," and "I have been tortured but have remained true to my ideals." If walls could see and speak, these would narrate numerous pathetic stories of sorrow, suffering, and hunger inflicted by the fingers of injustice. I could appreciate how these prisoners felt and could well understand why some of them had turned traitor. God's love is the only positive antidote to fear, and it was fear that had transformed many into traitors.

I began to wonder who it was that had slept in this stinking cell before me, and the sorrow of their burdens engulfed me with a strange sadness, filling my eyes with stinging tears.

"Dear Lord," I sobbed, "these sufferings happened right in front of Your eyes, for You never miss a thing. Their pain must have moved You to tears just as it did when You walked the windswept roads of Samaria and Judea. Thank You that You feel the pain of all mankind, that You enter right into it just as You did at the cross."

I felt the gentle Holy Spirit soothing my sorrow and for a while even my body ceased to feel the cold and hunger as I worshiped God in heavenly languages and praised Him in song. I imagined Paul and Silas singing songs to Jesus in the miserable conditions of that Philippian jail that would have been no more than two hundred miles from here. My soul was elated in God and I felt honored that He had permitted me, one of the least of His brothers, to be initiated into His sufferings. The words of an old hymn sang through my mind and broke upon my lips . . .

> Jesus I my cross have taken,
>   All to leave and follow Thee;
> Destitute, despised, forsaken—
>   Thou from hence my all shalt be.
> Perish every fond ambition—
>   All I've sought and hoped and known!
> Yet how rich is my condition—
>   God and heaven are still my own!

I had preached numerous times on the cross of Jesus but never until this moment had I entered into its mystical meaning. Here, in the baptism of His sufferings, in the beatings, the hunger, the cold, the sorrow, and the injustice, I had actually sipped and tasted something of the bitter wine that He had drunk to the dregs. It was not the cozy, comfortable cross that preachers sometimes glibly referred to. It was heavy, sticky, and blood stained. A cross where man painfully nails his old nature and then shouts to the universe, "I am persuaded, that neither death, nor life, nor angels, nor principalities, nor powers, nor things present, nor things to come, nor height, nor depth, nor any other creature, shall be able to separate us from the love of God, which is in Christ Jesus our Lord."

In some aspects life here in the Central Prison was easier, but only in the sense that the continual harassment of interrogation was over. Physical circumstances were definitely worse and the food no better just when my body needed extra energy to combat the freezing cell conditions. Winter was setting in, and with a broken window above my head, the temperature inside my cell could hardly have been any higher than what was outside. In fact, I found that it dropped as much as sixteen degrees below zero; even my urine in the toilet bucket froze solid. I have never known it so cold, but then the cell was on the north side and Sofia was high above sea level; furthermore, I had never had to try and keep warm in summer clothes before. My body was so cold that there were moments when it went completely numb; other times it ached, and there were even instances when I felt that I was stiffening into a death torpor.

The nights were the worst, for the intense cold frequently robbed me of the sleep that I so desperately longed for. On awakening after brief periods of sleep I was never certain that I was even alive. The new issue of three thin blankets did little to conserve any warmth; subsequently the exposed parts of me literally froze. My jaws began to lock and my head would throb for prolonged periods. The icy air even began penetrating my eardrums, resulting in excruciating pain and deficiency of hearing. But throughout the frozen nightmare, I was conscious of the Lord sustaining me. He knew exactly how much I could endure, for on one occasion when the pain and cold seemed too much to bear, I suddenly felt as though I was standing beside a burning bush out of which a cloud of radiant heat emerged to protect me from the cold.

December dragged by slowly, and naturally the weather did not improve. Sometimes I succeeded in mustering together enough energy to run and jump around my cell; I found that this exercise helped considerably in preventing my feet from freezing, for I was only wearing summer sandals.

Although we were forbidden to write to relatives and close friends, they were allowed to bring us clean clothes once a month in exchange for our dirty ones. We did not meet them; the exchange took place via the guards. If I had tried to contact them, maybe by a letter tucked between the washing, the note would have most certainly been found, for the guards were meticulous in their search.

I was most eager to get a message out requesting warmer clothing, and especially more blankets, but I also realized that I would have to be extremely cunning in doing it. To try and outwit the guards gave my mind something fresh to think about in the freezing conditions of my cell. Finally I hit on an idea. If I could embroider my request as discreetly as possible on a handkerchief, it might not be noticed during the militia's close inspection of my washing. Anyway, it was well worth trying.

I started looking around for materials that could be improvised for embroidery, and finally ended up tearing an old hand towel to pieces until I had sufficient threads. Although white in color, they were quite thick; this would not attract the attention of the militia but would hopefully be seen by my friends sometime during the washing or ironing. No needles were available so I made holes in the cloth with a small nail that I had found, and then poked the threads through the holes. It was exacting work for the intense cold made my fingers unresponsive. I also had to be alert for the guards who would tend to burst into my cell at any moment of the day or night without warning. So, with all my difficulties, it took me over two weeks to complete my embroidery, the simple message being, "Here I am cold and hungry; please bring me warm clothes and shoes."

My message got through undetected and a reply came back the same way: "Not allowed!"

I felt discouraged and was sure that the cold would eventually kill me for the temperature seemed to be dropping lower and lower. My head ached from hunger and my chest became so heavy that I increasingly had difficulty in breathing.

At times, however, the awareness of God's presence was so real that I experienced an indescribable joy resulting in temporary insensitivity to my sufferings. But just as there were sacred times so also were there long grinding periods of prolonged pain. Looking back now I marvel at how I managed to survive that penetrating combination of intense cold and gnawing hunger. It was a heavy cross to carry, yet a glorious one.

In Bulgaria we celebrate Christmas Day on January 7, but while many thousands of Christians made preparation for the joyful remembrance of Jesus coming to earth as a tiny baby on December 25, the Lord had prepared a special Christmas celebration for me. It happened quite early one morning. I was standing, feeling very low and sorry for myself but at the same time praying earnestly to God: "Lord, You once declared that although a mother can forget her child, You will never forget me. Please remember me at this approaching Christmas time. Here I am dying of cold and starvation; please help me or else snatch me away to Yourself."

Suddenly it seemed as though my cell disappeared as the scene of a vision swept through my scanty room and even beyond, for it seemed as though the west wall of my cell swung open and I found myself on the outside! Dark blue voluminous clouds were gathering on the distant horizon pushing their way across the entire length of the angry sky. A terrific storm was on its way for I could hear the distant rumbling. Directly in front of me stretched a pathway lined either side by graceful centuries-old trees. The path headed toward a large city spread open like a tablecloth beneath the distant yet oncoming storm. I remember that as I gazed at this panoramic view, my distinct impression was that this must be the coming of the Lord.

Then, in my vision, the approaching storm appeared to swing round and head back along the path toward the city. As it did so, its fury increased, wrenching up giant trees by their roots and hurling them effortlessly to the ground. On reaching the city, it smashed houses down one after another as though they were matchwood.

I was conscious that although being a spectator to all this I was nevertheless very much a part of it. I cried out to the Lord, "What does it all mean?" And at that moment out of the midst of the dark mass of clouds, a single burning white cloud appeared in which I saw the enchanting face of the Lord Jesus gazing down at me? "The storms will come and go, spreading havoc all around you," He said, "but you will remain safe; you will not be touched." As He spoke in what was an indescribably lovely voice, I was instantly aware of myself standing on a rock, in fact, almost one with the rock, and looking across the landscape again, I saw that the violent storm was gradually being swallowed up by a beautiful red cloud that appeared in one corner of my cell. It expanded rapidly until it filled the entire room enveloping me as well, and then it vanished as quickly as it had come, leaving me with an overpowering sensation of warmth and peace.

The nerves of my frostbitten body were tingling with life, and the physical warmth that the vision imparted to me remained for two weeks until the Lord provided for me in a different way.

It continued as cold as ever in Cell 219, but my heart was warmed in praise to God who had proved His love to me yet again. He had not let me down, and I knew that He never would, so I sang and praised Him from the depths of my heart.

I do not know if my friends were persistent in pressing for food and clothing to reach me, but eventually, at the end of December, two large suitcases full of clothes and two baskets of food were handed to me by the militia. Doubtless my sister-in-law living in Sofia had something to do with this and probably other loving friends, too.

At the same time the prison diet changed also. Now I was given as a main meal not just watery vegetable boilings but actual soup. This was followed by a substantial main course as well as a dessert. All my needs were suddenly being catered to. I was even brought a small mattress stuffed with straw by one of the guards. How wonderful to have a warm soft bed after hard bare boards!

It can be rather hurtful to question people's motives for doing you a kind turn, but after six months of suffering and deprivation I could not stop myself thinking that this sudden humane treatment must have sinister overtones. I put the question to one of the guards and his reply was blunt and simple, "Your case has been arranged for February so you won't be starved until then. From now on you can receive food and clothes."

So this was their game. Clearly my trial (along with that of others) was to receive international attention. To their astute thinking it would never do to let the world see how they really treated their prisoners.

The knowledge that I was gullibly taking part in their political hypocrisy gave a bitter taste to the food, but at the same time I knew how much my body needed it so I continued eating what they gave me, and my gaunt body gradually grew stronger as I absorbed the vital nourishment it so critically needed.

Days were wheeling by much faster now and news of the forthcoming trial plus the improved prison conditions began giving me fresh hope. Soon it was January 7, Bulgaria's Christmas day.

Suddenly they moved me from Cell 219, which faced north, to a similar room on the far side of the same block, Cell 216 facing south, and it was here that I saw the sun for the first time in many months. How blissful just to lift my haggard face to the single grimy window and feel it bathed in a gentle warmth!

On that same day a second delivery of food and clothes arrived from the outside world, and how my soul leaped for joy when, tucked away among the clothes, I found a small New Testament. It had been a long time since I had read God's Word. I had had to depend upon recalling portions of Scripture previously memorized and eventually this had become very difficult to do in the freezing conditions of Cell 219. Now I possessed a copy of my own and I clutched it to my heart with grateful anticipation. Many profitable hours were spent in reading, studying, and memorizing that New Testament. On retrospect, I am glad that I did, for it helped prepare me for further unforeseen circumstances ahead.

Christmas day was certainly a delightful one. I sang and prayed, absolutely overjoyed in the Lord as I recalled the blessed Christmas angels singing, "Glory to God in the highest, and on earth peace, good will toward man."

With more nourishment in my body not only did I feel physically better but I became aware that my mind was becoming more alert. Fresh thoughts and new ideas began nudging me into action. I began to realize that there were fellow prisoners on either side of the wall to me, living human beings that I needed to communicate with—but how? We soon discovered a way. By numbering the letters of the alphabet we found that we could tap out words on the wall by giving the appropriate number of taps with the necessary spaces in between. We called it "wireless telegraph"! And, although lengthy in operation, it nevertheless enabled us to effectively communicate with one another. To give an idea of the time that it takes to "say" things by tappings: "How are you?" in Bulgarian requres forty-eight taps, and all the pauses too. However clumsy this communication system may appear to be it certainly passed the time away as we spent many enjoyable days getting to know each other and passing on important pieces of information.

To my profound surprise, my neighbor on the right, after the usual greetings, tapped out his name as Pastor Jontso Drenoff. What a thrilling discovery, for Jontso was a close friend of mine who, up to the time of his arrest, was the pastor of the Evangelical Church in Varna, a coastal town on the Black Sea just over one hundred miles from Russe! Until tapping out his name through the wall, I hadn't realized that he had even been arrested. Jontso remained my neighbor throughout the months of January and February, and it was through him that I received much information about our impending trial. He informed me that fourteen pastors besides myself were imprisoned in Sofia's Central Prison, and the authorities were preparing a major case against each of us.

He told me the names of all the pastors—my brother Haralan was one of them. Jontso also explained that each of these pastors had been forced to give false statements of alleged spying activities on the understanding that confession of "guilt" would reduce their punishment. I was appalled at such outrageous injustice, to have to confess to something you have not done in order to soften punishment you did not deserve to receive. It was nothing more than a twisted plot propounded by the Secret Police. Why didn't they come clean with the fact that they hated active Evangelical Christians and that we were to be condemned as such, instead of all this nonsense about spying? I knew the answer to my own question. Since the attention of the world would be on this case, we puppets had to be dressed up to look good in front of the international press. So we were instructed to tell our relatives and friends to bring our best suit, a clean shirt and a tie. I refused. Although my body badly needed the extra food that they had been giving to me, I nevertheless could not play along with such pretense and hypocrisy.

Chapter Six

CRISIS IN THE COURTROOM

In December 1947, Georgi Dimitrov, Prime Minister of the Bulgarian government, pushed through a new Constitution for the People's Republic. One clause in this constitution guaranteed freedom of conscience, religion, and religious rites. It also forbade the preaching of racial, national, and religious hatred as well as prohibiting the manipulation of the church for political ends.

Things looked reasonably bright and tolerable, but in June 1948 the government of Bulgaria sent a directive to all church leaders laying down emphatically what was expected of them. It had four main points. They were that all church leaders should (1) not criticize the government, (2) support nationalism, (3) acknowledge that the state stands above the church, (4) support fully all government measures and train theological students to fulfill obligations to the government. In addition to this, the government insisted that because church leaders were respected members of the community they should therefore join the political Fatherland Front as examples to the people, and in doing so insure that: (1) they counteract anti-communist and anti-Russian propaganda from the pulpit and church press, (2) they display portraits of government leaders in their churches, and (3) preach love for state leaders.

Exactly what was it that the government was after? In the meantime they had arrested fifteen active Evangelical pastors, imprisoned them for six months and were now about to try them for crimes they had never committed. International press agencies had quickly picked up the story that immediately placed the Bulgarian government under substantial pressure to show the world that its hands were clean even if they were anything but clean.

The Deputy Foreign Minister and Press Director, Vladimir Topencharov, explained in a press release that, "Complete religious freedom is guaranteed by the constitution. The Evangelical ministers will be tried for specific crimes to which, in a preliminary investigation, they fully confessed."

On February 20, 1949, it was announced that Vassil Ziapkov, Chairman of the Congregational Churches and leader of all the Evangelical congregations, had confessed to a number of subversive activities.

Similar press releases stated that Dr. Georgi Chernev, Chairman of the Pentecostal Churches, was arrested "during an attempted escape into Turkey," and that six of the fifteen detained pastors were accused of receiving foreign money for their intelligence and subversive activities and then selling the currency on the black market.

To insure success in their trumped-up charges the authorities not only had us fifteen pastors imprisoned, they also detained certain selected "witnesses." In all, 170 people were interned in the Central Prison of Sofia, and on all persons who had needed to be "worked on," they had applied gruesome methods of coercion that resulted in fourteen of the fifteen pastors now being ready to confess to being spies. In fact some were ready to confess to almost anything, for their wills had been pulverized into complete submission.

As news of the allegations filtered across the world, many who heard it were horrified. A number of American pastors who had visited Bulgaria just two years previously understood the implications of such allegations. They had visited Bulgaria in 1947 as part of a concerted effort to bring relief to the churches, supplying us with candles, books, paper, Bibles and even funds for reconstruction work. In doing this they had naturally come to know a number of us quite well and lasting friendships were formed. They would have undoubtedly realized that espionage was just not on the list of our activities. I knew that in their eyes it all pointed to the forcing of our wills and the breaking down of our resistances by the authorities. Applying pressure and influence they eventually moved the American State Department to lodge an official protest at the "blatant terroristic efforts" to intimidate the religious denominations. The protest was handed to the Bulgarian Embassy on February 24, only to be rejected within the hour.

Later the same night, guards took all of us from our cells and drove us in cars to the Regional Court of Sofia where the trial was scheduled to begin the following day.

Sofia's official court building is a most impressive structure; in fact, it is the largest building in Bulgaria, tastefully furnished with mosaic murals and stern-looking marble figures.

We were directed down to the basement where we were given a cell of our own and a bed with actual springs! What luxury after months of sleeping on the floor.

The authorities were absolutely determined about the outcome of this trial, not only that we should be effectively gotten rid of, but also that our names should become a perpetual abhorrence in the eyes of the Bulgarian churches. On the day before the trial Mr. Timev, the Deputy Minister of Justice, released a vast document of two thousand, two hundred and sixty pages containing statements and depositions of our guilt. One can only assume that the reason it ran to such lengths and was released only one day before the trial was that the court officials were purposely not intended to read it but merely to be aghast and amazed at the enormity of our "crimes."

February 25 dawned, the morning of our trial, and one by one we were escorted up to Court 11, two policemen per person. Court 11 is not only the most important assembly hall but also the most charming. One entire wall is taken up with a marble mosaic of the goddess of justice sitting blindfolded, a sword in her right hand and a pair of scales in her left. Although aesthetically attractive, it was certainly not representative of the justice that we were about to receive in this trumped-up trial.

Row after row of solid-looking wooden seats crammed the hall, enough to seat more than 500 human beings. I noticed that nearly every place was taken. Special admittance cards had been issued to our relatives but the honored guests were the foreign press. It was for them and their readers that this farce was being performed.

We sat in the front center rows, and although separated from each other by policemen, we were nevertheless able to acknowledge one another with a casual nod. While everyone was settling into their seats, I gazed around me noticing the excited group of journalists and film cameramen on one side of the room, and of course the Secret Service men were there in the front rows of the far side.

It was carefully arranged that we each appeared in court smartly dressed, and I guessed that by now we all looked in reasonably good health, because the marks of our ill treatment had nearly vanished.

The judiciary consisted of three judges—one Chief Judge, a Mr. V. Omdjief, and two assistants who were merely powerless figureheads.

Moments later the trial began and, after a few preliminaries, Dimiter Georgieff, the Chief Prosecuting Attorney for the whole Republic of Bulgaria, stood to his feet and read the charges against us.

We listened intently, unable to speak to each other and not even daring to want to. Following Georgieff's deliberations we were quietly led back to our cells to await our individual appearance before the judges.

The first to step into the witness box was Baptist Pastor Nickolai Michailoff. He was first in line because the militia had broken him to such a degree that they knew he would say anything they wished.

Pastor Michailoff had been the President of the Supreme Evangelical Council, but now he gave his evidence helplessly. Choking back his tears he confessed to collecting certain information from pastor associates about military production, the coal mining industry and the placement of Bulgarian and Russian troops along the southern frontiers. This information, he claimed, was handed to a Mr. Cyril Black, the former secretary of the American Legation in Sofia. He explained to the packed courtroom that he was convinced that "the historic moment had now come for communism." He went on, "Today I feel proud of the Bulgarian Communists and the government." He was also careful to comment on how well he had been treated during his detention, and he refuted all allegations of torture. "My cell was rather small," he admitted apologetically, "but it was certainly not a torture cell. The Security Service made a new man out of me." It was evident that Nickolai Michailoff had been all but destroyed.

His hearing continued for six hours after which Pastor Janko Ivanov took the stand. Uninterrupted for over five hours he mouthed considerable evidence about his supposedly corrupt activities, but I suspect that few people really believed him. It became most distressing for his family and friends. The only ones who might have believed him were the foreign press who naturally knew no better. They were only just beginning to learn about the devious activities of the Secret Police. As with the other pastors who had been broken, Janko used meticulously prepared notes for his speech—the authorities made sure of this for they had planned on everything running as smoothly as possible.

Ivanov spoke of having been greatly influenced by the Americans and that he had made a serious error in imagining that the communist world had become the enemy of religion. He spoke in considerable detail regarding the intelligence activities of both himself and his collaborators on behalf of the Americans in 1944 and 1945. He admitted to large sums of cash being passed on to his sympathizers each month, the amount depending on the relative responsibilities of their tasks.

Janko also referred to Mr. Black, the American diplomat, and how he had given him 160,000 leva for certain confidential information. It was quite amazing how his story tied in with Pastor Michailoff's confirming practically everything he had said.

During the fifth hour of Ivanov's testimony the court was abruptly adjourned until the next day. For the D.S. it had certainly been one of undisputed success; for us, the prisoners, it was the beginning of growing gloom and despair. Surely the Lord would allow justice to be seen in this desperate situation? But like the passing unexpected appearance of a blazing comet, annoying questions flashed across my mind as they possibly did in the tired minds of my colleagues. Maybe God was powerless in this atheistic court? Maybe His hands were tied after all? I knew that He saw us in our helplessness but I was confused as to what He could really do about it. On reflection, I guess that even the holiest saints and apostles were plagued with those vicious moments when a temporary lapse of faith occurred. It was a dark time for us all. I despaired about the apparent suppression of truth and yet at the same time I sensed that God had everything under control in spite of the fact that as far as I could see He was doing nothing about it.

Early the next morning copies of our national newspapers were purposely brought down to us—how odd that the authorities had never been as thoughtful as this before! The main feature stories of course described the appalling admissions of the spy pastors. Public reaction, so they claimed, was adamant that maximum penalties should be heaped on them. It was asserted that we had sold the Republic of Bulgaria to the British and Americans and therefore deserved severe punishment befitting our crimes.

Later the same day, February 26, Pastor Vasil Ziapkoff was escorted from his cell to the court-room. The Secret Police anticipated that they would not be able to trust him to play along with their hypocritical game and this was their reason for placing Michailoff and Ivanov in court first. But Vasil did not let them down; he confessed at great length to collusion with Britain and the United States, explaining that now he was grateful to the communist authorities for making a new man out of him. Like Pastor Ivanov before him, he almost pleaded for punishment.

As I read the newspaper reports the following day I could hardly believe that these were the men of God I used to know. I hasten to add that I am not condemnatory of their actions for these are my Christian brothers, some of them close friends in the pastoral ministry. I know now as I knew then that their last ounce of resistance had been shattered by intimidation and torture. Every one of us, including myself, were broken men, and it was because of their brokenness that I continued to love them.

Monday, the 28th, dawned, and my brother Haralan was among those compelled to stand before the critical gaze of the court. He too had been callously manipulated by the D.S., and like the other pastors before him admitted to allowing foreigners to use their influence in spreading false political propaganda. The charges against him were quite ludicrous. For example, my brother was accused of passing on information to the Americans via another pastor about the unloading of one of our boats in the harbor of Bourgas (as if the authorities did not know about it themselves).

And so the entire farcical procedure dragged slowly on, while in the cells below the court I nervously awaited my own turn. At last, after all fourteen pastors had delivered their "pre-recorded" statements, I was summoned to the courtroom under police escort. The date was March 5, one that I will never forget, for from that moment I was on my own. I climbed the few steps into the brightly polished witness stand and after the murmur of voices had subdued the Chief Judge began his questioning.

"Pastor Ladin Popov, do you agree that you are guilty?"

"No!" I replied, and I was aware that my voice was raised to something approaching a shout.

Obviously annoyed at the bluntness of my answer the Chief Prosecuting Attorney stood to his feet and hastily addressed me with a second question.

"Your brother, Haralan Popov, has confessed before this court that you have been supplying him with spying information. Which of you is the liar, you or he?"

Once more I was conscious of replying in a loud clear voice, "He is!" I knew only too well that my brother would not have said anything of the sort. They were testing me with their lies.

It was at this point that the court seemed to explode into life, particularly in the section occupied by foreign correspondents. Cameras began flashing and popping and the buzz of voices interrupted the heavy silence. I knew that it could only have been the Lord who had given me the courage to answer like this.

The three espionage charges brought against me were as follows: (1) supplying information about gasoline storage plants near the railway station at Russe, (2) reporting about the behavior of people from Dili Ormona, and (3) supplying information concerning happenings in the railway station.

I desperately wanted to explain to the court that I had no idea where the gasoline storage plants were. Furthermore, if anyone really was interested about how the folk in Dili Ormona felt, surely the local pastors would be more reliable sources of information. During my five-year pastorate in Russe I had visited their area only three times. As to the apparent episodes at the railway station: on the few times that I had traveled from Russe to Sophia it had always been at night, and therefore too dark to see anything.

I asked the Chief Prosecuting Attorney for permission to explain to the court why these accusations were untrue, but my request was refused. Instead, I was ordered to speak of my involvement with a man named Leon Nadler. I explained that during the war most of the Jewish families had found it necessary to evacuate the capital city. Our church building in Russe had sufficient room to accommodate several of the families and did so. In return for this service, Leon Nadler, a wealthy Jew whom I knew quite well, paid our group of churches a sum of money with the understanding that a similar group in America would pay the same amount to certain people in Brazil whom he had named as beneficiaries.

At this point the Chief Prosecuting Attorney accused me of trading foreign currency on the black market, to which I was forced to plead guilty even though this had never been my motive or intention.

He then proceeded to label me as a homosexual and degenerate, neither qualifying his statements nor allowing me to vindicate my innocence. Having been unsuccessful in making the spy charges stick, he shamefully used the fact that I was unmarried to defame my character.

I delivered a short prepared speech before returning to my cell. "I repent and promise that not only will I refrain from such crimes in the future, but will be an honest, conscientious and faithful citizen of the Bulgarian Republic."

I had in God's strength made my stand, trusting that the watching world now realized that their crazy accusations were nothing but lies. The following day western radio stations proclaimed me a hero, and that same night Pope Pius XII held a special mass for the fifteen suffering pastors.

Even the witnesses called on to verify public accusations against us had been carefully primed into giving false statements. They blurted out feeble stories requiring considerable adjustment if they were to produce any real evidence at all.

One engineer working in a marmalade factory declared that a moderate sum of money that he had happened to find between the pages of one of his books had obviously been placed there by a visiting pastor with whom he had discussed the vacuum packing of marmalade. Another, the owner of a screw factory, insisted that he and one of the pastors had frequently discussed various aspects of engineering together. This was the caliber of accusatory evidence that was hurled at us—little more than lies and half-truths loosely strung together in an effort to sound convincing. I do not blame these men, for considerable pressures had undoubtedly been put on them.

By the time that all the witnesses had been heard, it was the turn of the Chief Prosecuting Attorney to sum up. He spoke for many hours propounding his political ideas rather than appropriate accusations. With great skill he set about convincing the court of how we had supposedly helped undermine the effectiveness of communism by preventing the workers from fighting for their ideals.

When Georgieff had finished, Taakoff, his assistant, started speaking. He lacked the diplomacy of his superior and launched into a barrage of insults insisting that we all deserved the death penalty for our crimes of espionage.

We were permitted lawyers to defend us but some of these were either paid off by the D.S., or they were put under such pressure as to find that their jobs were in jeopardy. Subsequently, their legal reasonings were anything but inspiring. In fact, they virtually reinforced the accusations made by the prosecution.

My brother had written to his wife requesting her to hire a lawyer to represent us both, and she was eventually recommended to a man by the name of Tomaroff who was not only one of the most widely acclaimed legal minds in Sofia but was also one of the few who were not members of the Communist Party. He agreed to take on our case, but his fee was enormous and quite beyond the reach of Haralan's wife. In order to engage him she was compelled to travel to Russe and sell many of my treasured books and household belongings. It was certainly not her wish to do this but in our present predicament there was no alternative.

"Your Honor," said Mr. Tomaroff with perfect decorum, "these pastors are being prosecuted as spies. Isn't it our task to find out exactly what their espionage consists of? And again, how does one define a state secret? Surely it is a bag into which you can put everything or nothing. Even a dead man can tell you that there is an arsenal near Kazanlik; everybody knows where it is. It seems evident in this case that a breach of state security is little more than what any diplomatic attache can find out when he goes to the nearest bookstall and buys himself some geography text books.

"For instance," he continued, "according to the words of the Prosecuting Attorney, Pastor Mishkoff had sketched a map showing a road from Plovdiv to Peschtera. He gave this to Pastor Ziapkoff, who in turn was supposed to have handed it to the Americans. Are the Americans so simple and uneducated that they would not go to Tshipeff's Bookstore (a large bookshop in Sofia) and purchase a map of Bulgaria? From this, they would not only receive direction from Plovdiv to Peschtera but also details of all our roads and railway lines."

Mr. Tomaroff had hardly concluded his speech when the Chief Prosecuting Attorney leaped to his feet bellowing across the courtroom: "Mr. Tomaroff! As a lawyer you have no right to say that! Don't you realize that everything is now secret in Bulgaria?" Seemingly quite unperturbed, our lawyer answered thoughtfully and perhaps prophetically, "Perhaps the day may come, sir, when you yourself will be in need of pastors like these." An impertinent answer perhaps, but at the same time I sensed that he had taken the hint for his later remarks brought him in line with the other lawyers who were supposed to be defending us.

Most of the lawyers advised us to plead guilty to the charges and beg for mercy. It was even suggested that we moan and groan in court, making a dramatic show of our sincere repentance, for this would enable the authorities to openly show their "forgiveness" and give a heavy prison sentence instead of the death penalty.

Some of the pastors did this, and of course the newspapers were quick to report it. "They have eaten and drunk and now they cry," splashed one headline. During this time, it seemed as though no public voice had a good word for us.

I guess that any astute political observer could have predicted the outcome of our trial. On the cool spring morning of March 8, 1949, our sentences were announced.

Pastors Ziapkoff, Chernoff and Michailoff, the main leaders of the Congregational, Methodist, Pentecostal and Baptist Churches, each received life imprisonment and confiscation of all their property by the state. A further four pastors, including my brother Haralan, were given sentences of fifteen years and confiscation of property up to the value of 250,000 leva (about $400/£200). Two more received ten years imprisonment, confiscation of property to a value of 150,000 leva, plus an additional fine of 150,000 leva. Yet another had ten years torn away from his life, plus a fine of 12,000 leva, and the twelfth pastor received a sentence of six years, eight months and a fine of 12,000 leva.

My sentence was five years imprisonment and a fine of four million leva (about $7,200/£3,600) which in those days was an impossible amount of money. This ridiculous figure reflected the alleged black marketing.

Two of the pastors were released on probation, but in the eyes of the state they were ruined men. From a political point of view, a trial spanning twelve days, consisting of seven sessions, each one dragging on for nearly twelve hours, and concluding with a one hundred percent prosecution, was a huge success for the D.S. Yet the trial itself was merely the climax of months of meticulous preparation by the Secret Police. They had staged it all, priming and even scripting the actors, reducing their resistance and breaking their wills to the point where they would say anything.

My brother Haralan later admitted that at the zenith of his sufferings, his mind was so pulverized by torture, that had he been told he had murdered his own mother he would have nodded his head in agreement. No blame whatsoever can be leveled at any of the pastors who confessed, for on top of all their physical and mental torture they had the worry of the well being of their wives and families. I only had myself to answer for.

Chapter Seven

TOGETHER AGAIN

From August 18 to March 8, nearly seven months, I had been a prisoner. It felt like a thousand years. Yet I had been fortunate, for many of the other pastors had been detained for far longer than this. Now that the trial was over and our harsh sentences passed, we faced the grim prospect of an agonizingly long period of imprisonment. For four, it was to be the horror of a lifetime.

To begin with, we were driven by bus back to the Central Prison in Sofia, twelve of us in all. For two of the fifteen, as I remarked earlier, were on probation, and Pastor Ziapkoff was taken elsewhere. We learned later that this poor man had completely cracked up. None of us saw him for three years during which time he was receiving treatment in the psychiatric clinic at Vratsa prison.

The security officers escorted us along dismal corridors to Department Seven on the fourth floor, and then divided us between three cells. Six of us shared Cell 213, Georgi Chernoff, Ivan Angeloff, Georgi Vasoff, Mitko Matteff, my brother Haralan, and myself.

This was the first real opportunity that we had to share our various experiences with one another so it was delightfully comforting to be together and recount what the Lord had brought us through.

Sofia's Central Prison was originally built to

house four hundred prisoners, most of the cells being intended for one person. At the time of our arrival, five thousand prisoners, both men and women, had been crammed in. The grounds of the prison, being quite extensive, contained separate buildings for housing the working prisoners, also a few workshops, a small factory and bakery, and the drab gray T-shaped cell block where we were incarcerated. Across the courtyard were tall observation towers containing the tiny moving figures of armed guards who never appeared to go off duty, and beyond that were the forbidding perimeter walls fifteen feet tall and three feet thick. Somehow, wherever I chose to look, the skyline screamed of our separation from the outside world—the only world that I had known. But we had all learned to our own good that it was never wise to brood over the horror of the past or contemplate the uncertainty of the future, just to live each day as it came.

It wasn't long before the authorities split us apart, and I found myself sharing another cell with Georgi Vassoff, Zakari Raicheff, Jontso Drenoff and Mitko Matteff. Mitko and Zakari were with us only two weeks, whereupon Mitko was transferred to a cell across the block where my brother was. In fact, it became a regular pattern for him to be swapped around from one cell to another, and it wasn't long before we discovered why!

Now that the trial had concluded and sentences passed, it was no surprise to us when our diets were drastically cut to a scummy soup and a few beans. Why should they waste good food on "spies"?

Cell conditions were anything but comfortable. Admittedly we had sufficient bedding, and winter was at last beginning to melt away into spring, but the warm sunshine began attracting detestable bed bugs that swarmed out at night to feast on us.

Thank God, we were allowed out of our cells twice a day, morning and evening, to empty our buckets, wash and go to the toilet. But even with these mild diversions, days became unbearably long, so we endeavored to spend a great deal of our time talking and praying together. Such fellowship inevitably refreshed our jaded spirits.

I began making contact with our neighbors by tapping on the wall just as I had done before the trial, but there was no response. Perhaps the unknown occupants were justifiably frightened of the punishment they would receive if they were discovered by the authorities. I then began tapping on the opposite wall and was overjoyed to receive an immediate reply. It was soon established by "wireless telegraph" that our neighboring cell housed seven young men who had been waiting two years for their execution to be carried out. They were in fact awaiting the death sentence for being members of the "Branzi" legionnaires, and understandably two long years of expecting to be hanged any day had frayed their nerves to breaking point.

The young man who did most of the communication was called Boris Strondjeff, a country boy from the charming little village of Kulata Vidinski, and like his six colleagues he had just concluded university training. I began wondering how these sad young men would respond to the gospel, so we immediately began praying that the Lord would prepare their hearts to receive the primitively transmitted news of Christ's love. Tapping out the simplest of messages is a lengthy business but I persisted, explaining to them about Jesus Christ, His cruel death on a cross of wood, and how we can be forgiven because of Him. It was thrilling, because the more I explained, the more eager Boris was to know about Him. Somehow in their deep gloom and hopelessness, Christ suddenly began appearing to these young men as their only ray of hope.

My friends Georgi and Jontso were now becoming enthusiastic about preaching with tin mugs and they too began tapping on the wall and "talking" with Boris and his cell mates. It was really elating to eventually hear from Boris that he and his companions had decided to believe and trust in Jesus. As days and weeks trudged slowly by, it became most gratifying to enjoy Christian fellowship together, and somehow those cold concrete walls that separated us suddenly ceased to exist. I even discovered through Boris that my brother Haralan was in the cell next to him, so here we all were, quite unknown to the guards, happily linked together in undisturbed conversation.

Mitko Matteff's condition was becoming an increasing concern to us. He was no longer interested in reading the Bible and sharing fellowship together; in fact, he became repeatedly antagonistic in our discussions and frequently contradicted our innocence when we talked about the trial. Whereas the other pastors were regaining their confidence and faith, Mitko seemed to be losing his. He had been so crushed and manipulated prior to the trial that a return to his former strong, vibrant and courageous self, in human terms, seemed an impossibility. I remarked earlier that he was frequently moved around from cell to cell. It was after one of his many visits to Tasseff, the prison superintendent, that we suddenly realized that he had become an informer. We learned later on that with the promise that things would be made easier for him he began reporting conversations and discussions that he was involved in or had overheard. State Security actually did shorten his sentence by two years.

Following something Mitko must have reported, my brother was taken from his cell one morning and beaten up. Georgi Chrnoff, Haralan's cellmate, tapped the news through the wall to

Boris and his friends who in turn informed us. On my brother's return after thirty-five days in the special punishment block, he was locked in the cell immediately opposite us with Ivan Angeloff, another pastor who had had to endure special punishments resulting from Mitko's reports to a security officer.

It was on an evening during this especially trying time that acute panic erupted in the cell next to us. Boris tapped out a hurried and evidently nervous message saying, "Tonight we have been dispersed into separate cells; I am left here alone. It is quite possible that this is the night of our execution." We were deeply concerned, knowing from experience that when the communist authorities are preparing for an imminent execution they always leave the prisoner alone in his cell. We prayed throughout that long night and right through the next day that the death sentence would be lifted. Occasionally we tapped out the gentle reminder to Boris, "You pray too," but understandably he was most discouraged, weeping profusely in his distress.

I was aware for many months now that he had been unable to go to sleep until after midnight (it was on the stroke of twelve o'clock that prison executions were performed). He had once commented via "wireless telegraph" that "Every night before sleeping I experience a horrifying feeling of execution."

The following morning we were pleasantly surprised when our cell door was unlocked, and the haggard shapes of my brother and Ivan Angeloff stumbled in. They had been cruelly treated but at least they were still alive. We told them of Boris's impending execution and that night all six of us prayed in earnest for the terror-stricken young man.

It was during that same evening while in prayer that I suddenly received a deep assurance from the Lord that Boris and his friends would not be hanged. I tapped out this conviction to Boris telling him that I had received it while praying. To begin with he remained doubtful, but later he tentatively clung to my words of assurance; they became his fragile wisp of straw to clutch hold as he was rushed along the dark river of fear.

Later that night we heard the familiar metal grating sound as Boris's cell door was opened. We all bolted upright on our bug-stained mattresses holding our breath in a mixture of hope and doubt. For some time we just sat there in silence listening to the dull drone of conversation beyond the thick grimy walls until once more there came that bittersweet open and close sound of the cell door. Immediately afterward hurried tapping began, and Boris's message was as follows: "We are acquitted! Without doubt the Lord is a powerful God. He saved us from death." I think we must have sung and praised the Lord all through that night for such an exciting answer to prayer.

Two nights later all seven young men were reunited in the next-door cell. We discovered afterward that during those two tense nights of waiting and wondering, the hair of some of those boys had turned white.

Directly across the courtyard and parallel with our section of the prison building, was the department where the women prisoners were held. They were granted more liberties than the male population of Department Eight, one of them being the occasional opportunity of reading daily newspapers. Since the women were aware that we received practically no news from the outside world, they often signalled across some of the more important news items. We called such news "partenka." Partenka was in fact the woolen material that the soldiers used for stockings inside their boots. To signal "partenka," the women spelled out words using their hands to form the shape of the letters. Boris was particularly gifted at communicating in this way so he would frequently pass on choice items of news by tapping them through the wall in the usual way.

On June 2 the women signalled across the stunning news that Georgi Dimitrov, Prime Minister of Bulgaria, had died while in Moscow. Although surprised, we nevertheless remained wary since much of the "partenka" that circulated our prison block consisted of false information leaked out by prison officials so that informers could report on individual reaction. That same day, however, Tassev prison superintendent came around for cell inspection. On entering ours we noticed a black band on his lapel and immediately concluded that the "partenka" must be true. We hoped that the death of Dimitrov would be to our good, possibly the easing of our prison sentences, maybe even our freedom, but such hopes were doomed to disappointment. The Lord undoubtedly had further purposes to work out in our continued imprisonment.

It was in that same summer of 1949 that three senior government officials became involved in a movement to create a federation of the Balkans with Tito. Georgi Dimitrov was one of them, and it was probably for this reason that Stalin had him liquidated. During this politically unsettled time the case of another man by the name of Traitcho Kostov was being processed by the Bulgarian authorities, and it was in this connection that all through one night we listened to tortured people crying and screaming as their hands and feet were burned. Three years later in the prison of Bourgas, I met one of these victims who showed me his ugly scars.

Kostov's trial came up in December of that year and a short time afterward he was taken away one night and hanged. I will never forget the year of 1949 as long as I live, for during that same month of December 200 death sentences were carried out. A third senior official, Vasil Kolarov, died of fear one month later. The governments of Russia and Bulgaria were becoming increasingly ruthless and we all began speculating on what would happen to us if the present trend continued.

In the middle of June the guards suddenly ordered us to pack together our few belongings and we were switched to a corner cell close to the exit of Department Eight. Although relatively large in size there was still very little room, for we were compelled to share the cell with twenty other prisoners. But it was during this time that the authorities began allowing us to take a short daily walk. What an indescribable joy just to step outside into the warm June sunshine, gaze up into endless blue sky and suck clean fresh air into our lungs! After long months of gazing at depressing concrete walls, an outside walk on a hot summer's day was comparable to a luxury holiday.

Once again, though, it was the bed bugs that became our major annoyance. There seemed to be indestructible droves of them that appeared daily to make a meal of our bodies. Some of us began wrapping ourselves tightly into any available cloth garment as a sort of anti-bug protection; this helped but it never stopped the creatures multiplying and pouring into our cell, especially after sunset when they became far harder to locate.

"Bed bug bruising" campaigns were not our only necessary pastime. At the conclusion of each day we would read the Word of God, share, and pray together. These became precious times that drew us closer to one another and helped the sorrows of our lives to become more bearable.

But Mitko Matteff, now one of our company, was becoming the cause of increasing trouble and pain. From the very beginning he made it quite clear that he disapproved of our Bible study and prayer times, and he was never slow in conveying his disapproval to the prison authorities. A few days later when we were all together in our cell, the door swung open and Tassev and his assistant, Jordan Chankoff, strode in. Addressing Pastor Lambri Mischkoff, they said, "Lambri, this is not the Bible College in Samdokov, yet it seems as though you are endeavoring to turn it into one." Shortly after they had left we were once more ordered to pack our meager belongings and were split into smaller groups and dispersed to separate cells throughout the prison. It was a profound surprise a few days later, however, to be visited yet again by a brightly smiling Georgi Tassev who politely informed us that we were to be given work, but first it was necessary that we become members of the prison "Cultural Society."

At the beginning we were relatively unsure of what the "Cultural Society" was really all about, and eventually, when its purpose became apparent, it was too late to opt out anyway. All prisoners were taken from their cells, stood in rows and one by one asked if they would or would not take part. I think most of us concluded that it would be to our benefit to at least fill out an application form. The officer in charge, a man with the grand title of Director for Educational Questions, ordered us into his office and in a "friendly" way gave some stern advice, recommending that it would be advisable for us to follow it. So we all became members of the prison Cultural Society.

It started off quite well really. The following day (for the first time) we were all given manual work to do. Some of us were carpenters, others bookkeepers, Lambri Mischkoff was a librarian, my brother a typesetter and printer, and the rest, like myself, were given employment in a cardboard factory.

Mingled with work the authorities organized choirs, theater performances, and lectures on Marxism, Leninism, agriculture and other subjects. Needless to say, it was the concentration on communism that revealed the true aim of the Society. The authorities were planning to inform us, or as they termed it, reorient us, and what better way than through a "Cultural Society"? No matter what subject the lecture was comprised of, our speaker always found an opportunity to extol Marx and Lenin, Communism's two most commanding figures. "Communism is the world's greatest political and humane system. Capitalism myst be totally destroyed," was the sort of glib phrase that regularly emerged out of those long summer lectures. Prisoners were in no position to contradict official dogma, for someone from State Security was always present. Disagreement with official statements was just not worth the trouble and pain that would inevitably ensue.

Some of the lecturers endeavored to justify the apparent uncertainty of their beliefs by constant repetition. Day by day, week after week they mouthed the same empty sentences in repetitive fashion. We put up with it for anything was more acceptable than stained gray walls and constant biting bed bugs.

I can still recall some of the incredible stories that our lecturers related concerning Stalin who at that time was still alive—stories that were told in the style of the fantastic tales from the Arabian Nights. Stalin, so we were informed, was the most brilliant man who had ever lived on earth, and also the hardest worker. As well as being the world's leading authority on the Russian language and Slavic literature, he also made a special point each evening before retiring, of reading two hundred pages from a book.

All the newly formed choirs were taught to sing songs about him and there was even a special cantata written in honor and glory of his name. I frequently questioned myself as to what kind of man Stalin really was, sane or otherwise!

Anyway, for most of us, reorientation by the Cultural Society proved to be a complete flop and waste of time, and before two months had passed Director Tschilchef himself had second thoughts about the success of his program. Only Nickolai Michailoff and, of course, Mitko Matteff responded favorably.

It was good however to have work to do but even in this it seems as though I could not fully satisfy the authorities. One day the workshop superintendent came and ordered me to be locked away in solitary confinement for three days. What for I do not know, for no explanation was ever given.

Not long after State Security had begun to realize how ineffective their programming of the Evangelical pastors was proving to be, they began sending us to different prisons in Bulgaria.

Lambre Mischkoff was first of all publicly criticized and then, a few days later, he disappeared. We learned later that he had been taken to the prison in Russe. Janko Ivanoff and Zdrauko Bezloff ended up in Varna's prison and so it was that one by one we were all transferred to various prisons throughout Bulgaria to continue our sentences. Only Ivan Angeloff and Zakari Raicheff remained behind in Sofia's Central Prison and probably this resulted from the high value the prison authorities placed on their skills. Ivan was a carpenter and Zakari a machinist.

On December 1, 1949, my brother Haralan was transferred to another prison, together with Christo Neitcheff, a Christian from a second trial of Evangelical pastors, plus about thirty other prisoners. A short time later during the same month, Georgi Vasoff and I were herded, together with another group of prisoners, and transported to our next detention center in order to continue our sentences.

Chapter Eight

EXECUTIONS AND EXODUS

To regret leaving prison may seem an odd thing to say, but in one way that is exactly how I felt when the fellowship with my good company of Christian brothers came to an abrupt end.

We left the prison in a truck, accompanied by a large and over-reacting group of guards. It was quite obvious that the responsibility of supervising such an assortment of prisoners not only made them edgy but also rather irrational in their behavior. As we clambered into the truck one young prisoner stumbled and fell, and immediately two guards leaped on him as he sprawled on the ground and savagely beat him into unconsciousness. The explanation given to their superiors was that they were under the impression that the prisoner was trying to escape. In our eyes this was nothing more than a feeble excuse for unprovoked sadistic behavior.

None of us had any idea where we were going as we traveled by truck and later by train. Someone grimly suggested a Russian concentration came which, if true, was a very ominous prospect. Eventually however our train pulled into a decrepit railway station now known as Vladimir Pavlov, and on being ordered to get off, we were gruffly informed that our destination was the nearby prison of Bourgas.

As soon as we arrived George Vassoff and I were separated, each being conducted to the punishment section of the building. As in other prisons certain aspects of prison procedure had jargon names which had degenerated into a sort of prison slang. Bourgas was no exception. The word for punishment here was "edinochki," and although I personally received very little "edinochki," the authorities certainly did all they could to wear me down. Doubtless the prison officials at Sofia had forwarded notes concerning my belligerent behavior at the trial.

Solitary confinement was the order of the day at Bourgas, and once again we got virtually nothing nutritious to eat, just the usual beans bobbing about in mildly flavored warm water. As a result of this I rapidly began losing the weight that I had gladly regained when the authorities had "fattened me up" for their courtroom farce. As the weeks of gnawing hunger crawled slowly by, I once more became aware of a growing physical weakness that I was powerless to correct. Occasionally my consciousness would slip away, and I would come to later only to realize that I had neither been asleep nor awake. This semiconsciousness would have been frightening had I not recognized that it was in fact a built-in safety valve assisting me to stay alive.

It was on New Year's Day, 1950, that I happily anticipated a temporary conclusion to my forced starvation diet. Marched out of my cell by a guard, I was conducted to Gunchev, the prison superintendent who, with what I detected to be a sly grin, informed me that my father had sent a food parcel and would I mind signing that I had received it. Of course I wouldn't mind! He must have known how my entire body ached for a substantial meal. With no hesitation I signed, and then waited in childish expectation for my food parcel to be opened for inspection. Folding the signed paper with deliberate unhurried ease, Gunchev slipped it into his pocket, opened a door behind him and shouted for two prisoners who I later discovered had notorious reputations for collaborating with the Communists.

As I stood there, the two prisoners were then ordered to untie the parcel. I could sense the activity of my salivary glands as they unwrapped fried pork, fruit, and fresh bread. But the delicacies never touched my lips for Gunchev stepped forward, handed some food to the two men, and between the three of them they unashamedly devoured the entire food parcel in front of my eyes. Rage and tears boiled up within me at their cruel and dirty trick. It was very hard to forgive them, and on reflection perhaps this was one of the worst tortures inflicted on me at Bourgas.

Time dragged by, but the Lord was as wonderful as ever. This time I at least had enough clothes to keep me warm in contrast with the agony of the previous winter. There were even blissful moments during six months of enforced solitude when the Holy Spirit entered my cell, filling me with an idyllic joy and peace. In fact, if leaving solitary confinement would have meant the loss of the delicious awareness of Christ's presence, I would have happily stayed there. But eventually those long months trickled to an end, and I was allowed to resume work again, this time in the prison woodwork shop where furniture was made. I will never be able to boast of acquiring a great skill in carpentry, but at least my pieces of furniture were functional, plus the fact they helped to keep my mind occupied.

As in the prison at Sofia, there were men here at Bourgas awaiting execution; for them, an opportunity to escape, however slim, was a risk well worth taking. But successful escapes were extremely rare for too little food inevitably meant that most of us were far too weak to attempt any strenuous activity. Two prisoners did try to escape during my stay there. They resided together in the same cell, both expecting execution any day. One was a farmer about sixty years old who went by the name of Bai Dragan. His colleague was a young circus acrobat whose name I never did find out.

During the six months of waiting for their death sentence to be carried out, they somehow managed to hack a hole through the cell wall that emerged right beside a drainpipe. How they did this with neither tools nor the guards discovering them will forever puzzle me. One night when everything was ready they crawled through the hole and slid down the drainpipe to the courtyard below. The young acrobat even succeeded in throwing the entire courtyard into darkness by ripping out the electric wires from a nearby fuse box.

Racing across the woodwork shop they dragged out several lengths of timber and propped them against the prison walls with the idea of using them as scaling ladders. But as they began their climb, they were spotted by a guard who opened fire. The younger man was hit in the leg by a bullet and in a matter of minutes both were captured and thrown into solitary confinement. The following night they were both hanged.

The actual execution was pitiful to watch. As they were led out to the scaffold, the older man, Bai Dragan, was weeping bitterly, calling out the name of his son again and again. "Velcho, my Velcho, where are you?" A rope was hastily strung round his neck and the battered barrel on which he was standing was kicked from beneath his feet. Velcho's father twitched two or three times and then wobbled to a standstill, dead! The acrobat was much more composed; he muttered a few indistinguishable words and bravely put the rope around his own neck. Needless to say, these two men became heroes overnight, but the public horror of the crude way in which they died remained in my mind for months.

One week later we witnessed an even worse

injustice that ended in an innocent man being executed. His name was also Bai; Bai Damian, a wealthy farmer who owned a large house in the city of Bourgas. He had been accused and charged with instigating a deliberate act of sabotage. Apparently, large amounts of hay belonging to the T.K.Z.S. in the tiny village of Bata had been deliberately set on fire. The T.K.Z.S. represented the local farming commune to which Damian had presumably refused to belong. The real arson offenders, who were also from Bata, had themselves been caught, and when questioned by the communist authorities about Bai Damian, replied in all honesty that they never knew him. It was at this moment that a loathsome bargain was struck, for the Communists offered the real offenders their lives if they would openly declare that Damian had masterminded the crime. The Secret Police could find no other way of hurling charges at an innocent farmer who was getting in their way. Bai Damian was sentenced to death and the three alleged accomplices received fifteen years imprisonment.

Bai was led out to his execution quietly repeating, "I am innocent, I am innocent," but of course, none of the authorities paid any attention to him. The executioner stuffed cotton wool into Bai's mouth, tightened the rope round his neck and kicked that familiar barrel from under his feet. The rope broke however and poor Bai Damian crashed onto the ground still alive. His hands became untied, and snatching the cotton wool from his mouth, he called out pathetically, "Look, even God will not receive me!" His confused executioners hurriedly got another rope, retied his hands and once more stuffed his mouth with cotton wool and Bai Damian was hanged again, this time successfully.

God gave me numerous opportunities to speak for Him during my stay at Bourgas, both directly and indirectly by my tapping on the walls. Inevitably I soon contacted people intent on a sincere search for peace and truth. It was a particular joy one day to be suddenly handed a Bible by another prisoner who, on cleaning out the director's office, had found it in the wastepaper basket. He knew how thrilled I would be to receive a Bible, so he smuggled the book out presenting it to me as a gift. I clutched the sacred writings between my fingers in sheer joy, feeling very tempted to keep every page myself in order to devour those living passages that had helped to sustain me in past days. Yet I knew that some of the newly interested friends that I had recently contacted would greatly benefit by having Bible portions of their own, plus the fact that separated into smaller parts they would far less likely be found by the guards. With these thoughts in mind, I divided the Bible into suitable sections and distributed them among the prisoners as opportunity arose, leaving myself with the book of Psalms. I grew to love that spiritual poetry book during the remainder of my confinement in prison and daily found myself entering into the very same feelings as the writer; his joys and laughter, his tears of despair, his ups and downs—they all became perfect articulations of my own changeable emotions under prison pressures.

One evening, just as we were relaxing after a gruelling day in the workshop, the prison authorities swept into our cell on one of their unannounced surprise inspections. There was nothing unusual about this appart from the fact that this time they found my cherished Book of Psalms among the few belongings that I possessed. I was immediately rushed to the office of the Chief Prison Director who on examining the worn pages asked, "Where did you obtain these enemy books?" Without even waiting for a reply he bellowed at the top of his voice, "And how dare you read enemy literature in this prison!"

I informed him of how I had obtained it, omitting the fact that it was only part of the complete Bible that I had received. I was not worried about mentioning the prisoner's name who had found it in the wastebasket, since he had already left the prison.

I should have anticipated by now that this man would refuse to believe my story. If I had strung together some incredible far-fetched tale, he would probably have beleived it, but the truth he angrily rejected. He began beating me, cursing God, the Bible, Protestantism—in fact, any religious idea that entered his head. Throwing me to the floor, he then commenced kicking me, and there was nothing I could do, except suffer it until he decided to stop. Eventually he did, and I stumbled slowly onto my feet again in profuse pain but at the same time conscious of an inner joy and confidence in spite of the brutal treatment that I had received. "Comrade . . . Mr. Director . . ." I gasped, trying to get my breath back again. "Please permit me to say one thing. I am quite ready to lay down my life for this same God and Bible for which you have so brutally beaten and kicked me. No matter what you decide to do, nothing will ever influence me to denounce Him, for even my death will only be a gateway to my being with Him."

Frankly I was both amazed and thrilled that the Lord had given me the courage to make such a forthright confession. Gunchev, the prison director, immediately responded by sentencing me to ten days solitary confinement, but even here the presence of Jesus was so real that I think I spent most of the time singing hymns. Solitary confinement was also an excellent opportunity for practicing "wireless telegraph." By now I had acquired a system beginning with a tapped introduction of something important that I wanted all my neighboring prisoners to listen to. Inevitably, someone would then tap back that they were ready to listen.

I then asked if they were true believers in Christ. Usually the answer was "No!"

"Have you heard that Jesus Christ died for your sins?" was my next insistent question.

This time their reply might well be, "Only in the Orthodox Church when we were children."

"Let me tell you then what Jesus Christ has done for you and what He longs to do in your life right now," was my further response. I would then tap out God's plan of salvation through the sacrifice of Christ.

Eventually the moment would come when some of my unseen contacts would tap back the following request, "A few of us are now ready to believe in Jesus. Please pray for us." I would then ask them to kneel down and pray, and I would do the same.

During successive "conversations" after their conversion to Christ, I endeavored to teach them, and in so doing, build up their faith in Christ. Although the process was laboriously long and involved, it was nevertheless an absolute necessity if they were to become mature Christian men. My concerted attention to their spiritual growth usually paid off, for many of these young Christians became devoted followers of Jesus, sharing an expanding faith with their cell companions and to anyone else to whom they could "tap" the Good News.

What with occasional work, Christian witness, singing and reading, the months were now passing much faster. God was so good to me; at times His presence was overwhelming. And on top of this He would frequently arrange exciting opportunities where I could speak of His love to many of the dispirited prisoners. A hundred times over I proved the reality of Paul's words that "all things work together for good to them that love God," and also in all honesty that a Christian can "give thanks in all circumstances."

I had been officially informed that my five-year prison sentence ran from the day of my arrest back in August 1948, and from that five years, three days were subtracted for every two days work that I had carried out in the prison. After simple calculations I felt a growing excitement at the thought that I might soon be released. At the same time, I endeavored to temper that excitement, telling myself again and again not to be stupid enough as to build up too many hopes that could suddenly be dashed to pieces.

September 15, 1952, is another one of those unforgettable days in the checkered history of my life. It was a crisp early morning at the beginning of autumn; friendly sunbeams penetrated the grimy window panes of my cell and played together on the opposite prison wall. Suddenly, a guard unlocked the door and the Prison Superintendent strode in. He informed me in a surprisingly friendly yet anxious tone, "Ladin, I want you to quickly pack your belongings together. You have served your time, and now we have to release you immediately. This should have happened two days ago, but circumstances forbade it. Hurry up now, we're late."

The sunbeams suddenly seemed brighter than searchlights. Tears of joy dripped down onto my poor prisoner's luggage as I hastily packed the few articles together. The same thrill that I felt seemed to permeate my cell companions also as they listened to the exhilarating news. I shall never forget them. Some were Christians while others still opposed the God they blamed for allowing them to be there. One or two even denied His existence altogether. Yet each man purposely hid his grief to share my happiness. I say each man, but there was one who continued to sit sad and thoughtful in a corner of the cell. He was sentenced to life imprisonment, and for prisoners like him, freedom came only with death. The declaration, "Pack your belongings together, we have come to release you now," would never be directed at this man.

Bittersweet feelings crowded into my mind. I was sorry to leave the friends I had made, but thrilled to realize that I was about to stride out into the glorious freedom beyond the tall prison walls. As I rolled my meager belongings together into an untidy bundle, my fellow prisoners gathered around me, shaking my hand, slapping me on the back, hugging me and even singing happy freedom songs. Five long, dark years of communist imprisonment had at last come to an end. Nevermore, I hoped, would I be shadowed by militia men or snarled at by prison guards. From now on I would walk unmolested down our busy city streets just as I had done in the old days. I planned on visiting my native village, and of course looking up my relatives and friends again. My happy anticipation was tainted by a degree of trepidation when I considered the many new adjustments that would have to be made. I began wondering how family and friends would greet the prospect of my need of a home, and to begin with, a little nursing of my frail body. I knew that I could no longer go to my father, who out of grief for my brother and I, had closed his eyes forever just one year ago.

Clutching my pathetic little bundle of possessions, the guards directed me out of the prison block only to leave me standing alone beside the two large and forbidding prison gates. After five years of waiting and longing, the relatively few moments of standing around while officials signed and countersigned handfuls of administrative papers, seemed unending and unnecessary. I then began to realize that they were, in fact, not for me, but for a dishevelled line of incoming prisoners straggling behind me. Secret Service men, like panic-stricken rabbits, began scurrying in and out of the chief jailer's office on official business. Their presence made me worry as to whether the authorities had changed their minds about my release. Maybe this entire episode was a sick joke or at the very least some chronic administrative error?

"Are you Ladin Popov?" said a curt voice, as the jailer stepped suddenly from his office with a heavy key in his hand.

"Yes," I answered. He thrust a bunch of release papers into my hand, turned the key in the iron gate and uttered a soft, "Congratulations!"

The gates swung open, and I made my exodus into the warm sunshine of the free world.

Chapter Nine

FROM FREEDOM TO FRUSTRATION

Stepping from blurred memories into the stark reality of things can be a rather traumatic experience. I certainly found it to be so on the day of my release from prison. I guess I must have looked quite a sight standing all alone on the pavement blinking my eyes in owl-like interest at lines of bustling cars, a cluster of laughing school children, and multitudes of men and women walking up and down the busy streets. Remember that I had not seen anything like this for more than four years, and now, quite suddenly, it all seemed somewhat unreal. Looking back now on that memorable day of release, my image of freedom will forever remain a muddled mixture of grumbling traffic, fresh air, and vehicle fumes. It was all so exhilarating, and my heart pounded with the blissful assurance that it all belonged to me.

Most of the people I stood gazing at took little, if any, notice of me, except for two elderly smiling ladies on the other side of the road who appeared to be nudging each other in mild amusement at my bewilderment.

I knew one of them quite well since for the past three years she had been attending to my washing and was always trying to bring in food parcels. I had even succeeded in speaking to her on two or three occasions. The other lady I recognzied as Marijka Stefanova, who was the wife of one of the deacons at the Bourgas Evangelical Church.

Snatching up my bundle of belongings from the pavement I crossed over the road to meet them, comforted by the welcome of their wide smiles.

"You will come and stay at our home," said Marijka, speaking first. "We are here to meet you and take you there."

"The Lord has truly sent you," I said falteringly, feeling hot tears pricking my eyelids. "He knew that I had nowhere to go since my dear father died, so He sent you along to provide me with shelter."

A sudden feeling of intense loneliness swept over me as I stood gazing into the faces of these two quaint ladies. For a brief moment I felt like a parentless child wandering lost and helpless in wide and unfamiliar surroundings, but my pain soon turned into appreciation as they gripped my arm and began chattering away to me.

We made our way down the street and across the city to the house of Josif Stankova. As Maria guided me through her front door, the sound of laughter and conversation quickly subdued only to revive again as the occupants (a large grinning group of Christians) gathered around to congratulate me on my release. Someone grabbed my arm, pushing me toward a table piled high with delicious food and fruit that had been carefully prepared as a thanksgiving for my release. But no one seemed in a hurry to eat. With tears in their eyes, every person in that room hugged me and welcomed me to freedom again. Instinctively, we all united together in prayer to thank the God of heaven for preserving me throughout the years of my imprisonment. And as we prayed and sang I think every person present became conscious of the blessed Holy Spirit brooding over us as if in celebration of my release. After that we feasted long into the evening.

Surrounded and protected by the loving care of these gentle Christian people I soon began to settle down and feel at home in Bourgas. At the same time I had no intention of becoming a burden to them in spite of the fact that, owing to my physical weakness, I felt acutely dependent on their help. Receiving many invitations from various Christian families to stay with them, I soon began moving from home to home; this helped lessen the load on individuals, and of course I always endeavored to help as much as possible around the house. But even this dissatisfied me. Being an active person with a revulsion for laziness, and now that I was daily growing stronger, I began looking around for some sort of employment. Apart from keeping me occupied, any money that I might be able to earn would certainly help repay the kindness of those precious people who had given me accommodation. Before long I began working for Dimiter Baselkov who was a builder as well as a member of the Bourgas church. My tasks were straightforward, not too taxing on my still weakened physical body, and of positive assistance in helping me to stabilize my life and adjust once again into a constructive kind of routine.

Perhaps most important of all, my new work enabled me to procure some money for my brother Haralan who was still in prison and would remain so for many years to come.

During my five years' absence, noticeable changes had occured in the structure of Bulgaria's Evangelical Churches, the most pronounced being the increased domination by communist authorities. Actual Party members as well as sympathizers were now compulsorily appointed as council members. The communist hierarchy evidently had a well-defined policy operating in connection with the running of the Evangelical Churches and I was determined not to lose my newfound freedom by becoming embroiled in the affairs of such a dubious administration. I went to church regularly, of course, making friends with the new Christians, enjoying the community fel-

lowship, and at the same time grasping any opportunity to share some of those unforgettable experiences that the Lord had given to me. This was
profitable for I at last felt that I was regaining
something that my caged confinement had
squeezed out of me. Like a newly released bird I
was at last finding that I could stretch my wings
and shake off the grimy dust of my imprisonment.

The Bourgas church was one of the largest
Evangelical Churches in Bulgaria, both in influence and size. Its pastor was Eduard Korian, an
Armenian by birth. Strange to say, we were both
the same age and had graduated together at the
same Theological Colleges in Danzig and London.
Even our ordinations had been performed on the
same day, November 7, 1938, by the Englishman
Howard Carter. It was remarkable that we should
suddenly be thrown together after all this time,
and as can be expected we spent many hours rem-
iniscing.

Eduard and the spiritual members of his
council approached me one day inviting me to take
over the youth work in the church. I was obviously
rather reticent to accept their invitation, mainly
because of possible interference by the authorities,
but I was discreetly informed that so far, the
Communists had not thrust any restriction on
youth activities. It was only the Sunday school that
had been forcibly abolished.

So I accepted their invitation, beginning as
youth leader over a group of about eighty young
people. Concentrated Bible study became my main
objective, and it paid off for the zeal of the Holy
Spirit began burning in these young lives and they
all started to win others to Jesus Christ. In a matter of months the number in the youth group doubled, and before long the figure surpassed two
hundred.

This was a tremendous thrill to the older
people in the church of course, but on the other

hand I sensed it produced a degree of insecurity with the pastor, my old friend Eduard.

It is not easy for people in the free West to comprehend certain pressures prevalent in a communist-dominated society, especially back in the fifties. No matter how well a pastor knew his congregation and felt one with their aspirations, there was always someone who could be persuaded by the authorities to talk. It happened at the summit of this revival atmosphere. With so many exuberant young people being influenced by what the Communists regarded as a direct opposite to their own ideology, they immediately stepped in. Up until this moment we had been conducting group Bible studies in various homes, but the authorities now made it abundantly clear that from now on this was strictly forbidden. Within a few days of this abrupt decision Pastor Eduard Korian was summoned to Sofia by the council that oversaw the group of Evangelical Churches of which Bourgas was part. It was not long after his return that Eduard invited me to his home, and on arriving there I immediately discerned that he had something serious to discuss with me.

"Ladin," he murmured after a prolonged silence. "I am very sorry to have to tell you this, but I was informed in Sofia that you are no longer allowed to work within our group of churches since you are not registered as a pastor."

I think I anticipated that this was what Eduard was going to say, but it still hurt me deeply. "But surely," I reasoned, "there is no need for me to be registered since I am not working as a pastor and I have no congregation. You know that I am just an ordinary church attender now."

"Of course I do," responded Eduard sympathetically, "but you must admit that you have a higher biblical education than the average church attender; they themselves would be quick to acknowledge this."

I nodded in agreement, admitting that this was true.

"You probably realize, Ladin, that it was the authorities, together with certain members of the council, that made this decision to curtail your activities among the young people. I endeavored to convince them that your sudden removal would have a devastating effect on the entire church but I'm afraid they would not listen."

After further prolonged discussion I concluded that the wisest move I could make would be to gradually ease out of my position as youth leader allowing Eduard to step in. My suggestion evidently pleased him and I was happy to see that it relieved him of some of the worry and tension he had been under.

Our mutual arrangement worked well to begin with until overnight the authorities suddenly clamped down even harder by forbidding all religious gatherings anywhere, except in the church building. The young people were extremely resentful about this ruling. Their resentment rapidly resulted in disillusionment, and in a matter of weeks the youth meetings came to a sad end. It was obvious that communist strategy had achieved its destructive aim.

The blissful freedom that I had been enjoying was linked to the presumption that the authorities were no longer watching me and prying into my personal affairs. It was some time before I discovered that this was not so, for during my remaining five years of residency at Bourgas, I began to be summoned regularly to the State Security building for questioning.

In April of 1955 I was once more ordered to report for questioning. On arrival at the glum-looking police building, I was immediately directed to a room where two inspectors, Colonels Sharlopov and Diochev, were waiting to see me.

I felt very much on edge, suspecting that this

time my visit was something more than routine questioning. Sharlopov evidently recognized how ill at ease I felt, for he kindly invited me to sit down. His first question, however, did little to calm my nerves.

"Comrade Popov, we have just received an anonymous letter complaining about you, and for this reason we thought it best that you came in for a little discussion. The writer seems most agitated about something; here, read it for yourself."

He casually held out the handwritten sheets of note paper between two fingers. I took them, scanned the paragraphs briefly and instantly recognized the distinctive handwriting. My immediate conclusion as to the identity of the writer shocked me. I didn't want to believe what I saw so I hastily rechecked in case it was a forgery, but everything according to my limited knowledge seemed to be in order.

"This letter is not anonymous," I retorted angrily, immediately checking myself, conscious of my raised voice. "It is written by Eduard Korian, pastor of the Evangelical Church here in Bourgas. I know his handwriting very well. We studied together at college for two years. I am absolutely certain that this letter was written by him."

"That was our conclusion as well, Popov, but why should he be so embittered against you and insist on your being expelled from Bourgas?" asked Colonel Sharlopov sharply.

It was all so bewildering to me, especially after the friendly discussion that Eduard and I had had together. We were friends; we had been for years. No, I just could not believe it of him. Maybe these two officials seated in front of me had engineered the entire situation.

"It is only Pastor Korian himself who can answer that question," I answered breaking the strained silence. "I have no idea why he has done this. Perhaps some outside authority has exerted pressure on him to write in this way."

Sharlopov was far too quick to allow my insinuations to slip by unanswered.

"Do you think then that we have forced Pastor Korian to write such a letter to you?" he quizzed.

"Why not!" I answered casually.

"You are wrong, Comrade Popov. That has never been our game. You can be assured that he has written it on his own initiative."

Sharlopov was insistent to the point of being dogmatic, yet how could I be certain that he was telling the truth?

"And if we didn't write the thing, it doesn't say much for the pastor, does it?" he added ruthlessly, snapping his fingers and pointing to the letter to indicate that I ought to begin reading it in detail.

Counting the number of pages convinced me that it was a lengthy letter that I needed to read immediately for it was doubtful whether I would be given another opportunity. But surely the inspectors didn't expect me to plow through it all while they sat patiently at their desks? Evidently they did, so I began reading, and what I read horrified and distressed me.

"Ladin Ivanov Popov, former Evangelical Pastor; address, King Boris 1st Street 66; appointed a glazier [a new job that I had taken] by the Construction Organization; he regularly attends the church services and is recognized as sympathizing with Western world powers. By his agitation among church members he incites them against the People's Regime. . . . Because of this the Supreme Council of the Evangelical Union has repeatedly reproved him, but Ladin Ivanov Popov has never given our admonitions any consideration, and for this reason we consider him to be dangerous to our town and kindly request the esteemed authorities to expel him from the area."

I felt bitter and resentful at this gross injustice. How could Eduard do such a thing to me?

Lifting my bowed head I looked into Colonel Sharlopov's face saying, "Tell me, comrade, do your really believe that all this is true?"

He thought for a moment and then gave an answer that was anything but profound. "The letter does appear to be rather overheated, I must admit, but it puzzles me just the same."

"I can assure you, Colonel, that this letter is a lie from beginning to end. There is not a scrap of evidence in it. First, you can contact the members of the Evangelical Church and see if any of them can prove that I have at any time incited them against the People's Regime.

"And second, why doesn't Pastor Korian mention a name in his letter so that the individual concerned can be called in to make his accusation in my presence?

"As for claiming that I have been repeatedly reprimanded by the Supreme Council for such activities, you can always check this by looking up their records. I say again that it is all a complete fabrication."

Sharlopov leaned back in his chair, stretched out his legs and gave a nonchalant sigh. "Yes, Comrade Popov, people are bad these days, but it's a great shame that there are such even among your crowd. You Christians are supposed not to lie and steal for isn't that what the Bible teaches? It seems to me as though your Christian teaching hasn't done much good really."

For a brief moment his words put me off balance, but then I felt a mounting sense of annoyance at his priggish and indifferent attitude.

"It is the likes of you who have made some of us Christians react like this," I blurted out, conscious yet again that I was raising my voice, "and now all you do is stand back and sneer."

Maybe they were risky words that I would have occasion to eat, but I was angry. The crooked strategy of communism was becoming increasingly abhorrent to me. I hated the evil way they planted distrust, suspicion, and disloyalty in the minds of the people.

Surprisingly enough, our conversation continued for at least another hour, but it was at the point of dismissal as I was walking toward the door, that the other inspector who had said very little throughout the questioning, called out a final suggestion.

"Hey, Comrade Popov! If you learn anything about Pastor Korian, write to us about it, and we'll pull his ears for you."

"Listen, Colonel Doichev," I said, turning around and looking him squarely in the eye, "never expect that of me. I know nothing bad of Pastor Korian, certainly nothing worse than what you can see." With that I left.

In the following months several incidents occurred between the authorities and myself that were suggestive of Eduard's increased manipulation by State Security. I no longer felt any bitterness toward him for I knew that his hurtful letter and change of attitude toward me resulted from growing intimidation. The police would not leave me alone either, for on a number of occasions I was arrested and even tortured by Security officers, and always for some vague, pathetic reason. It wasn't long before they expelled me from the town of Bourgas and for the next ten years I wandered from village to village, never able to settle anywhere owing to systematic harassment by communist authorities.

Life had certainly become very difficult. On the day that I stepped onto the freedom side of those iron prison gates I foolishly imagined that all my suffering, misery, and persecution would be behind me forever. But this was not to be. It was evident that I had underestimated the power of the People's Regime! Bulgaria was no longer the land of freedom that it used to be. The fate of my dear brother was also hanging heavily on my mind but at least I was able to help support him. Although moving from village to village, my new profession as a glazier always seemed to be in demand, thus providing an adequate salary to look after myself and my brother cramped away in a faraway communist dungeon.

Chapter Ten

"WELCOME HOME MY BROTHER AND GOOD-BY!"

Life had been agonizingly hard for my brother Haralan. He had experienced suffering too monstrous to imagine. During the thirteen years of his imprisonment he had been hustled around from one torture camp to another, the worst being the island of Persin, near Belene. It was here in the wild north of the country beside the gently flowing Danube River that winters were inconceivably terrible. Prisoners were reduced to devouring anything that was remotely edible. Grass, dogs, cats, snakes, and rats all helped to subdue their raging hunger pangs. Amid such demoralizing conditions, savage guards would shoot down prisoners who were caught scrapping anything consumable from the fields where they were working. Many of the friends that my brother had made on the island of Persin died there, emaciated and broken in mind. Yet the Lord chose to preserve Haralan, and it was from Persin that he was eventually released.

It was early on the morning of September 25, 1961, when the copper-colored leaves were beginning to fall from the trees, that the barbed wire gates of Persin prison swung open in front of my brother. Seated forlornly in a horsedrawn wagon, he watched for the last time his cell mates shuffling into the fields under armed guards on another day's backbreaking labor. With a sudden jolt, the cart lurched forward over the flimsy island bridge to prison headquarters in Belene and from there to freedom.

Having experienced myself how embarrassing it can be to step into freedom dressed in ragged, threadbare clothes and worn-out prison shoes, I had taken the precaution of forwarding some money to Haralan in order that he might purchase necessary items. Although stepping onto what proved to be deserted streets at 8:00 that morning, he still could not bring himself to buy clothes and shoes, so strong was his fear of the possible presence of the Secret Police.

At the railway station in Belene he found that he had missed the train by one hour. The next one wasn't due until the evening. In an agony to get far away from the area he started off at a brisk walk, continuing like this for about six miles until he sighted a bus that he hastily boarded. At 2:00 in the afternoon Haralan arrived at the small town of Krasno Gradiste, and found his way to our uncle's home where we had both spent many of our early years. Two days later we both met, embracing each other with tears of joy after thirteen long, lost years of inhuman separation.

Haralan had still not purchased new shoes. In fact, by the time of my arrival he had hardly stepped out of the house. For three months he remained like this, absolutely refusing to venture outside for fear that the Secret Police might be following him. Eventually, as his lost strength and confidence revived, he began accompanying me for short walks around the nearby villages, including the one where we had built a house for our parents.

It deeply concerned us to see how deserted the streets were. Many of the houses had been abandoned entirely, including the one that we had built so many years ago. In reply to our questioning my uncle claimed that everyone in the district was kept forcibly working for the communist collective "Grape Kolchozen." Most of Bulgaria's grapes came from the large vineyards in this vicinity, and since the young people had already moved away to the cities in search of better employment, local work requirements were inevitably forced on the remaining occupants of the community. It saddened us to tread across those barren streets that had once rung with noise and laughter. The house where we once lived, that we had built with our own hands, now stood desolate and decrepit. The old barn and stable had completely collapsed and both were gradually disappearing, together with our beautiful orchard, beneath a sea of choking weeds.

Over the next few months my brother had the opportunity to visit some of the churches he had known before the trial, but he was distressed to find that in many, the flame of enthusiasm had burned very low. In some areas communist authorities, in a wild effort to decimate congregations by prolonged persecution, had ejected the people from their church buildings, forbidding the subsequent formation of house meetings, and banished the pastors to distant towns.

Thank God, Haralan had domiciliary rights in Sofia and was therefore permitted to live there, but procuring acceptable accommodation proved to be a near impossible task. Eventually he succeeded in finding a small attic room above a church meeting hall. Although no larger than the cells we had spent our prison years in, with a bed, a small desk and a chair, it at least provided him with a degree of privacy.

In November, 1961, Haralan became the pastor of an Evangelical Church in the suburbs of Sofia. To begin with, it consisted of about fifty elderly people meeting together in a private home, but God blessed my brother's ministry and the numbers multiplied as young people began flocking in. Needless to say, this did not escape the notice of the authorities.

In the hot July of the following summer, a dozen local Party leaders attended one of the meetings, afterward explaining that as members of the community they had come to complain about the church's teaching against family responsibilities. This unreasonable accusation had in fact originated from the wife of one of the congregation, a Communist Party member who had never attended the meetings. Because no one was successful in proving any of the allegations, the authorities unhesitatingly used their final trump card—the church was sadly informed that they were no longer permitted to meet in the house. There was little they could do about this decree except unite with a similar church in the city of Sofia.

From the moment of his release, Haralan had requested permission to emigrate to Sweden in order to rejoin his wife and family, but his pleas were constantly turned down. Haralan's wife had even traveled to Bulgaria, spending the best part of two days waiting at the office of the Ministry of Internal Affairs, hoping to discuss her husband's request with the minister. This too had been useless.

One tiny spark of hope gleamed in my brother's heart. In the attic room next to his lived a Christian lady by the name of Maria, who was continually reminding Haralan that while she was in prayer God had clearly told her that Haralan would make it to Sweden. But as the months slipped by, the miserable trend of events seemed to entirely contradict this.

A letter arrived one day ordering Haralan to visit the office of the Ministry of Internal Affairs. On arrival he was gruffly informed to stop requesting permission to leave Bulgaria and to write to his wife and tell her likewise to stop bothering them. They explained emphatically that, owing to his prison record, he would never be granted permission to leave the country, and in the process be given the pleasurable opportunity of relating his story to the press.

Naturally this utterly depressed and disillusioned Haralan. On relating his experience to Maria, she responded by laughing, telling him that the Ministry knew nothing, especially about God's power. Her trust in what she believed God had revealed to her never once wavered.

People frequently imagine the Lord as having only limited control over the multiple incidents of our lives, failing to realize that He can wrench entire nations to their knees in order to accomplish His purpose. If this is true then it was easily in His power to engineer radical changes even in the government of Bulgaria, which in fact did happen as a result of the Communist Party's annual conference. Among the many political changes was the replacement of the Minister of Internal Affairs.

It was inevitable that the years of harsh imprisonment had, for many of us, impaired our physical health and strength. The predominant disability was the weakening of the heart.

On December 28 we learned that our dear prison companion Janko Ivanoff, the Methodist pastor, had died of heart failure. He had been the last of our group to be set free and had spent only three precious months with his family before the Lord snatched him away into Paradise. I attended his funeral, which was at the First Evangelical Church. In spite of it being an official work day, the number of Christians attending the service was most impressive. There were few dry eyes on that cold winter morning at the graveside.

Afterward I accompanied my brother back to his attic room. Awaiting him, tucked between the gap under his door was a thin but important-looking letter.

I was standing at the top of the long flight of stairs when the yell of "Passport! My passport to

110

Sweden!" resounded from his room. I nearly fell backward down the stairs in astonishment as he handed me the note to read. "Please report to the Passport Office. Your passport to travel to Sweden has been granted." This sounded too impossible to be true. Experience had taught me to be very cautious, so I added rather lamely, "Don't get too excited, Haralan. Something still could happen to you." But when Maria was told, she just smiled sweetly and said, "I knew it would happen." For my brother it was a miracle as profound as birth.

Haralan wasted little time. He raced down to the Ministry of Internal Affairs and they immediately requested 32 leva for a new passport that arrived at his attic room the following morning. Neither were there any problems when it came to obtaining a visa. With this, his passport and a flight ticket, he was ready to fly on Monday, just three days after receiving that thin, important-looking envelope.

It was while Haralan was waiting for the final stamp on his Bulgarian passport, that he was directed into a very plush office labeled "For Foreigners." It was in this room, a few nervous hours before his departure for Sweden, that an important-looking government official remarked at length: "Comrade Popov, you have been imprisoned for many years. It was we who condemned you, though we know now that you were innocent at the time. But many of our mistakes have had to be committed to the past, not only relating to the trial of you pastors but also to our own Communists. Like you, many of them suffered unjustly in severe prison conditons for crimes they never committed, but all this was during the time of Stalin. Stalin made many mistakes, one of which was your trial. Now we have new politics and have therefore decided to let you go to Sweden in order that you may be reunited with your family. We have families ourselves and know exactly how it feels to be separated from them. We are giving you a passport that is valid for only six months, but don't worry about this. We realize that you will probably stay there with your family, but we will nevertheless be happy for your to return here whenever you wish, and afterward to return to Sweden."

After everything he had suffered, Haralan was understandably surprised at the genuineness of this official, but as for returning? Political changes are both questionable and unpredictable in communist countries. To return would demand a great deal of thought.

I accompanied Haralan to the airport. It was 10:00 on the foggy morning of December 31, 1962. At 10:40 the Lord swept aside fog and cloud, and the sun slanted through like a warm spring day. I watched as Haralan's plane became a rapidly disappearing speck in the sky. "God go with you, my brother, God go with you," sang my heart in profound relief for the freedom of one who had suffered so monstrously.

When I could see the plane no more I turned toward home, hot tears pricking my eyelids. It was as I stepped outside the airport building that I noticed how quickly the fog had once more descended, this time more dense and dark. Haralan had gone, and I was alone once again facing a very uncertain future.

I returned to my daily employment with a construction company, while in the evenings I helped organize small secret house meetings for Christians. I traveled many miles from village to village preaching and ministering to people, many of whom would walk great distances in order to enjoy Christian fellowship in someone's home.

The fact that I was constantly on the move and that Haralan was now residing in Sweden were the twin factors that introduced a further ministry for the Lord—the distribution of Holy Bibles. From time to time my brother would mail me copies that I was able to distribute among Christians who did not possess a Bible of their own. This became a marvelously gratifying job as I saw joyful expressions appearing on their faces and listened to the overwhelming thankfulness pouring from their lips. Sometimes they would even jump for joy and smother their new Bible with kisses.

By 1966, Haralan had so organized things that he was able to direct the printing of large quantities of New Testaments. The spring and summer of that same year saw me distributing 1,500 copies, and with others doing the same thing, a total of 2,500 New Testaments passed into grateful Christian hands. Although exciting and encouraging, it was but a drop in the ocean of the vast need for Bibles and Christian literature that had emerged since the communist takeover some twenty years before.

Chapter Eleven

GRANDPA EFTIM
AND GRANDMA DAFINA

In 1964, I too began applying for permission to leave Bulgaria, but at every application, permission was refused. Unlike Haralan, I had no wife and children in Sweden.

On May 4 of the same year, I was once more summoned to the office of Ivan Sharlopov, the agent that I had previously confronted at the Bourgas regional office of State Security. He curtly informed me that I must leave this district forever, including all the neighboring villages where I would also have no right to settle down and live. This was a shattering blow. It was one thing to be nomadic in accommodations, but now, with banishment from the district, my employment was snatched away from me also.

I packed my bags and left for Sofia, later moving to Russe, where I was welcomed into the church fellowship of a warm and affectionate group of people. It was here that I once more became involved in church activities and the people appeared delighted that I should do so. It wasn't long, however, before I was called yet again to State Security office to be questioned by Intelligence Officer Ivan Donchev. He told me all that I had heard on Bourgas; that I had no legal right to live in the town since I was not a citizen, neither had I any authority to preach in the church since I was not officially registered as a pastor. He then ordered me to be out of the town within fourteen days.

On asking why, Donchev repeated his accusation. "Because you are not a resident of the city."

"But I know numerous people living in the city who are not residents either," I replied. "Why then are you hounding me now that I have just begun new employment here?"

Unable to logically answer my simple question, Donchev lost his temper and shouted back, "Listen, Popov, I'll repeat my order to you for the last time. You are absolutely forbidden to work in either this city or this country."

"Yes, Sir, I hear you," I replied as politely as possible. "But please look at things from my side. I have been forbidden to work in Bourgas, and now it is the same here. If I move to another place, a similar situation will be sure to reoccur there. Where am I to live and work? Can you not see that I am being forced into an existence of hunger and misery?"

Not so much as a glimmer of sympathy showed on his face. He stared at me, cold and aloof. "That is not my worry, Popov. You must obey my orders. If not, you will face another five-year prison sentence. We have orders for you to leave Russe. Make sure you are away from here in fourteen days."

I moved back to my native village of Krasno Gradiste. Living here at least enabled me to work among the neighboring churches of Pavlinkeni, Kutsina, P. Kosovo and Trojan. Most of these had no official pastor, so for two years, I was able to assist the local leaders in preaching and visitation.

The fact that I had been officially banned from entering the district of Bourgas did not, however, prevent me from brief return visits.

I desperately needed to return for there was an elderly couple, Grandpa Eftim and Grandma Dafina, living in the city who had always been exceptionally kind and loyal to me. Because of this, I had grown to love them dearly.

They lived at Zar Boris 66, where they had

built a large new house with their life savings. Behind this new house was the old one that they once lived in, but it was now occupied by a number of young families, one family per room, under the jurisdiction of the Communist Rent Control Court. Connecting the two buildings was a narrow annex that housed Grandpa Eftim's old donkey, its fodder hay, and the old couple's winter wood store.

This couple's contented lifestyle, their peace of mind, and their pleasant-looking property was the envy of many of their neighbors. They were a quaint and simple-living pair; neither could read or write, but neither could they be easily fooled.

On the outskirts of the city were fields full of vineyards, and it was in this area that Grandpa Eftim owned a small plot of land that he had transformed into a vineyard and vegetable garden. He would spend the long winter months with his donkey, carting manure and preparing the ground for the spring when he and his wife would plant an interesting variety of vegetables.

This old couple were virtually inseparable, whether at home, working on their small plot of land, or riding their donkey cart along quiet country lanes. They lived for each other, spending their lives showing warm Christian hospitality to the steady stream of men and women who called at their home each evening.

On reflection, I always imagined that the old couple were so godly and attractive that people found themselves unable to resist the charm and spirituality of their lives. Like our Lord, people were magnetically drawn to them, not only because of what they said, but for what they were.

Grandpa and Grandma had three daughters and a son. Two of the daughters were married while the middle one, who was deaf and mute, remained at home. She, like her dear mother and father, was a Christian, hardly missing a church service and was always to be found sitting eagerly at the front.

If their deaf and mute daughter could be considered a hardship, Grandpa and Grandma had a further frustration, one that constituted profound sorrow to their hearts. It concerned their only son, whom they had not seen for many years. He had managed to escape to the West, and their only contact with him now was through the occasional letter that they received. "I am well here," he would write. "Don't worry about me. We will be together again soon." Letters like this always brought fresh hope, but then there would be the inevitable four or five months of silence that produced great sadness and anxiety in their minds.

During my ten years of suffering and persecution, this protective Christian home became a comforting refuge for me. Not only was my soul spiritually refreshed, but there were many times when the old couple literally saved my life from the Secret Service agents who always seemed to be pursuing me.

Sometimes while staying overnight in their home, Grandpa Eftim would visit my room, and leaning on the doorway, utter a great sigh. "Ladin, why haven't we received a letter from my son? What is happening that would prevent him from writing to us? It is six months since we last heard from him."

"Nothing has happened to him, Grandpa Eftim," I would reply. "Your son is happy and free. Don't worry. You know how young people are; they just don't think."

Grandpa was frequently interrogated by the Secret Police about his son who, before his departure to the West, had been the personal chauffeur to our late King Boris III. When the Communists took over the country, the boy made his successful escape after growing persecution from the authorities.

117

They wanted to know where he was of course, but Grandpa would never let on that he had been hearing from him. He was even able to deceive them into thinking that he had disowned his son and knew nothing of his whereabouts.

One day, without any warning, old Grandpa burst into my room and leaped about waving a letter in the air. Almost as if singing in an opera, he sang, "A letter from Pieko! I have a letter from Pieko, my son!"

"Calm down, Grandpa," I said with a laugh, "or you'll be falling through the floor in a moment."

Apparently, this song and dance routine occurred every time one of his son's letters arrived. It was a joy to share in his joy however, for this dear couple deserved the abundant measure of happiness that they unconsciously handed out to others. Grandpa Eftim and Grandma Dafina became the source of unending inspiration to numerous people, and it was in their home that many young people confronted Jesus Christ for the first time.

Years swept by. Then one day, Grandpa Eftim was informed that his small field and vineyard had become the property of the People's Government. This was a crushing blow to the old man. He knew that it would be useless trying to argue his case with the authorities, so he sold his donkey and cart, and with the money, purchased a bicycle for his grandchild. After that he spent increasing hours trying to keep busy in the backyard of his house.

It was while he was working around his house one day that two Secret Service men opened the gate and entered his backyard uninvited.

"Good morning, Grandfather Eftim, and what are you doing these days? Surely not working at your age? Remember that you are not a young man any longer. You should take things easy and rest a little more."

"But doesn't our government teach that if someone refuses to work they should not be allowed to eat?" replied Grandpa with polite sarcasm.

Inside he was angry, but at the same time he was too cunning to show how he felt. It was these very people who had robbed him of his livelihood. Who did they think they were, telling him not to work?

"Listen to me, Grandpa," continued one of the agents all too casually. "Is Ladin here?"

"Who is Ladin?" replied Grandpa innocently.

"Don't play dumb with me," the agent retorted angrily. "You know very well that we refer to the Protestant pastor who lives with you."

"Why do you want this man? What wrong has he done to deserve such constant persecution?"

"That's none of your business, old man, and if you refuse to let us know if Popov is here, we will make it very hard for you too."

Extremely annoyed, Grandpa Eftim quickly responded to their crude threats.

"Who do you think you are to yell and harass me in my own yard? Do you think you are gods just because you happen to belong to the Secret Police? You had better move off right now . . . and don't come back again!"

"Calm down and don't get excited," interrupted the second man who up until this moment had hardly uttered a word.

"Why should I?" responded Grandpa. "You insist on harassing a lonely, innocent man. Look at the number of times you have arrested him. Aren't you ashamed of this? And then you tell me to calm down and not get angry!"

The rough-speaking agent tried to quiet him, warning him to watch his mouth unless he wanted to end up in prison with other enemies of the state.

"Who, me?" shouted Grandpa at the top of his

voice. And scurrying into his little barn, he returned some moments later brandishing an axe. He found no one around though. They had anticipated his intentions and made a quick departure.

Racing to the gate, he shouted after the two figures rapidly disappearing down the street, "You want to arrest me, do you? I'll kill you first, and I have a strong suspicion that the Lord will forgive me for doing it!"

Still muttering, he returned to his work as I continued to peep out of the corner of a small nearby window behind which I was hiding. I marveled at this old man, who would sooner risk imprisonment than expose me to the communist authorities.

I continued to watch him for a few minutes. It was as if nothing had happened. His hammer kept up a steady rhythm while birds in nearby trees returned to singing their songs in the watery spring sunshine.

"Grandma Dafina!" called a voice at the door.

"Sister Koino, is that you? Come on in," answered Grandma from her favorite chair where she sat absorbed in her knitting. The door opened and Sister Koino sauntered in. Not only was she a neighbor, but she also attended the same church as Dafina. Grandma was quite used to seeing her in her home, since Koino would drop in several times a day. This time, however, she seemed to have something special on her mind. Seating herself near the window, she began speaking in a rather demonstrative and demanding way that suggested she should have Grandma Dafina's entire attention.

"You must ask Ladin Popov to leave your home, Dafina," she insisted in the same persuasive voice. "Don't you realize that he is a dangerous man who can bring you nothing but trouble? The government is highly suspicious of your son, and permitting Ladin to stay in your home does little to

120

help the matter. " She continued with her cutting criticisms, concluding with the advice that I ought to be thrown out immediately.

"Listen to me," responded Grandma Dafina defensively. "I have never seen anything wrong with Brother Ladin. We believe him to be a fine Christian man. What right have you to speak out against him when you do not know him like we do? I fail to understand you, Sister Koino. You have been influenced by someone—maybe the police.

"I certainly will not ask Ladin to leave. Is this what Jesus teaches us to do, especially to someone who has suffered so much?" Without another word, Sister Koino left and returned to her house.

By the time Grandpa Eftim entered the room, Grandma had quietly resumed her knitting. She related to him what had happened, to which he replied, "If I ever see her again, I will forbid her to enter my house."

Neither of the dear couple wished to worry me over this incident and for some time they diplomatically refrained from mentioning it.

It was shortly after returning from yet another discouraging visit to the State Security office, that the incident was accidently mentioned during conversation.

"Grandpa and Grandma? In the eyes of the authorities, I am a dangerous man. I am considered to be a threat to this city, and I therefore feel it right that I should not risk your lives any further. I will leave this area in the next few days. Please pray for me, and I promise that I will be back to visit you as soon as things quiet down."

They protested my decision of course, but my mind was made up. I could not bear to think of any harm coming to Grandpa Eftim and Grandma Dafina.

Chapter Twelve

"FLIGHT TO FREEDOM"

On February 21, 1966, I filed yet another application to leave Bulgaria and join my brother in Sweden. The previous year I had developed a rather worrying heart condition and had mentioned it to the authorities in my application, hoping that it might somehow provoke added consideration of my request. Haralan and I were in constant touch with each other by letter, and he had made repeated requests through the Red Cross to gain consent for my release. My own application was held for one year. Finally, the answer came back: "Your petition has been denied."

I was amazed at the incredible stupidity of the authorities. What on earth did they expect me to do? I could get no work, my health was failing, and I was forbidden to visit many of the towns where my friends were living. Hunger, misery, and death spread out before me as my inevitable future. On the other hand, I knew that God would never let me down. He had taken care of me before, providing everything that I needed, and He would undoubtedly do it again. I had much to praise and thank Him for.

It was near the end of June, 1967, during one of my return visits to Krasno Gradiste, that a Christian friend approached me, looking very perturbed. "Ladin, I must tell you something that you must promise never to repeat. If you do, I cannot imagine what might happen."

I nodded reassuringly, and she continued. "Yesterday, I was in Pavlikene and accidentally met Comrade Jordanov, the head of the Secret Service. He questioned me at some length as to your whereabouts and your present occupation. I told him everything I knew, adding that you are a well-respected friend in the village. At this point, he became extremely angry, and as I listened to the things that he had to say about you, I was afraid—afraid for you, Ladin! You must go far away from here, and as soon as possible."

I thanked this dear Christian lady for her brave kindness and hastily returned to the house where I was staying. After packing my bags, I traveled to another town a few miles away. The Christians here received me warmly, and fortunately I was able to register in the town and receive a medical certificate that was an absolute necessity if I was to remain there for any length of time. However, it turned out that I did not stay long, for a further consignment of Bibles had arrived and were awaiting my attention at Sofia. So off I went again, distributing these through the various church contacts around the country.

With all the running and hiding that resulted from Bible distribution, it was of absolute necessity that I keep in close touch with the Holy Spirit's leading. He became my eyes and ears of hidden human events.

It was while I was sleeping in Sofia on the night of September 26, 1967, that I was suddenly awakened at 4:00 in the morning. In a clear voice the Lord told me to leave the city, and in simple obedience I hurriedly packed my bags and boarded a bus for another town. A couple of hours after my departure, two militia men from the Secret Service burst into the houshold to arrest me. My host informed them that I was not there and proceeded to ask them why they were looking for me.

"That's none of your business," was the brash

reply. "And we will search this house anytime we like."

A similar situation occurred in October when I was traveling in the direction of a friend's home in Sofia. On arriving in the city, around midday, I suddenly had a deep and definite impression that I should not visit this home. Recalling what had happened before, I turned in the opposite direction toward the house of my cousin and her husband with whom I had not stayed before.

In the late evening of the following day, I boarded a cross-city bus in order to make a brief visit to the friends whose house I had been strangely steered away from the previous day. I knocked on the door but no one was in. Maybe I should not have come after all, and perhaps my "impression" of the previous day was little more than a figment of my imagination. Anyway, I decided to practice precaution and make the return journey by train. While waiting on the platform, who should I see but the daughter of the friends from whose house I left! Flushed, out of breath, and with a look of fear in her eyes, she said, "Uncle Ladin, how long have you been in Sofia? We did not know you were here. Only this morning two agents from the D.S. called at our home looking for you. My mother told them that you were not here and that you had left Sofia two weeks ago. They refused to believe her and accused her of hiding you. So she opened the door and invited them to make a search. As you can well imagine, they left in an angry mood."

At this point, my train steamed into the platform and our conversation was forced to an abrupt conclusion.

Once more, panic and foreboding swept over me like stormclouds across the sun. My future was black and dangerous. What should I do, and where should I go? Life had become a fugitive existence with no castle of protection to run to.

I spent most of the night in prayer to God, and in faithfulness to His promise He answered me, for I distinctly heard him say: "Get up! Take the road that you have often given careful consideration to, and go now, for danger is following you at this very minute!" He went on to comfort me with the thought that He had already prepared the way ahead.

On October 8, 1967, the border between Yugoslavia and Bulgaria was opened in observance of a holiday, and at the border cities of Kalotino and Dimitrovgrad, little formalities were involved in crossing the checkpoint.

I knew about the date of this border opening as far back as the beginning of the year, and had subsequently arranged to meet Rhoda, Haralan's daughter in Dimitrovgrad on that day. We had been able to make arrangements through her husband who, as a doctor, had come to Sofia for a medical conference.

The authorities had since altered the date of October 8, and in haste I sent a telegram to Sweden in order to make the necessary change of arrangements. Regrettably, this led to some confusion.

At 3:00 in the morning, taking nothing but my umbrella, I walked to the railway station with my cousin and her husband. They were simply planning to cross the border into Yugoslavia in order to purchase some European goods that were unobtainable in Bulgaria. They had no idea of my plans. The train was scheduled to depart for Kalotina at 5:30.

I recalled the charming story in the Book of Acts of how an angel had spoken to Philip the evangelist, saying, "Rise, go south to the road which leads to Jerusalem through the desert of Gaza." This is how the Lord spoke to me, the only difference being I was heading west. Philip was commissioned to take joyful news and enlightenment to the Ethiopian, and I was being snatched out of the clutching fingers of the enemies of God's Word to continue a ministry in the West.

The Jews, slyly plotting together to kill Paul, watched the city gates day and night waiting for the moment of opportunity. Secretly, his friends hoisted him down over the wall in a basket and he escaped. Now, when the Communists had succeeded in closing all the homes to me throughout Bulgaria, God provided a way of escape—not in a basket but in a train!

Meanwhile, Rhoda had traveled from Sweden to Dimitrovgrad, and was waiting for me at a mutually planned location.

That same morning, I reached the Bulgarian border accompanied by my cousin and her husband. Thousands of people were crossing unchecked into Yugoslavia, and all I had to do was mingle among them. By 8:30 I was in Dimitrovgrad. The danger that had threatened me for so long was hopefully coming to an end. But where was Rhoda? She was nowhere to be seen at our preplanned meeting place.

I waited for a while, panicking, but praying. Then I crossed the street to a line of taxis having decided to hire one to the town of pirot-Nis, and then on to Belgrade. Just as I was speaking to the driver, I felt a hand rest gently on my shoulder.

"Uncle? I have been looking for you. Where have you been?" To my overwhelming joy and relief, it was Rhoda. She had likewise just arrived, and after our unfortunate confusion in communication, was wondering which way to go. How precise is God's timing! He had directed her to me in spite of the many thousands of people crowding into the fair.

On reaching Belgrade, there followed many frustrating hours trying to procure help from the United States and Swedish Embassies to get me out of the country. But there was a marked reticence on the part of the authorities. My prison record made me an extremely risky person to deal with, and they were not prepared to take any chances.

In desperation, dear Rhoda took me to a villa belonging to a friend of hers. It was beautifully located on the shores of the Adriatic, in Pulla, near Trieste. I remained here for two weeks, revelling in the sunshine and freedom, but at the same time very worried as to whether I would really escape from the communist bloc.

On the unforgettable evening of October 21, Paul, Haralan's son, and his friend arrived. I called them the "two angels," not from heaven but from Sweden. They had at last been able to obtain permission for my entrance into their country and were now about to snatch me away forever into a land of complete freedom.

Early on the following morning, we left the villa and drove to Trieste, and from there, two hours later, we arrived at the Yugoslavian border town of Kopur. This was the final danger point, but the Lord had everything under control. There were no problems, and we crossed the border singing, "Redeemed, redeemed forever from the hand of Communism."

At 2:30 on October 22, I arrived at Haralan's home in Sweden. Praise to the Everlasting, most powerful God! My long fugitive days were now over—I had entered into the long-awaited dream of freedom.

The publishers invite correspondence regarding the present situation in Communist lands. Gifts for printing Bibles and assisting suffering Christians in Communist countries may be sent to—

Rev. Haralan Popov
Founder
Evangelism to Communist Lands - USA
Box 303
Glendale, CA 91209

ECL - Canada
Box 65899
Vancouver, B.C.
V5N 5L3

ECL - India
Box 223
Woriur, Tiruchirapalli
India 620003

ECL - Australia
Box 230
Moe, Victoria 3825

ECL - England
Box 66
Southampton S09 7EL

ECL - South Africa
Box 4073
Pretoria 0001
Rep. of South Africa

PLEASE CHECK CORRECT BOX BELOW:

☐ Please inform me regularly about Christian news events in Communist lands. Send me the *Door of Hope* magazine free of charge for six months.

☐ I am willing to share this book, enclosed find $_____ for the payment of _____ copies.

☐ Please print below:

Name _____

Address _____

City _____

State _____ Postal/Zip code _____